PRAISE FOR *AMAZING RACE*

Amazing Race explodes out of the blocks the gold. Filled with sound wisdom that a leader needs, *Amazing Race* will not only touch your heart and soul but will have a profound impact on your leadership journey. Dr. Banks crafts leadership lessons that transcend sport. Not only do the stories honor my 1968 teammate but will move you to maximize your potential as a leader.

—Dr. John Carlos,
1968 Bronze Medalist 200 Meters,
USA Track and Field Hall of Fame
and US Olympic Hall of Fame

Amazing Race communicates the timeless testament of the power of one person. When love, faith and rare leadership genius is embodied by a track coach, the results can be generationally transformative. With surgical precision and poetic brilliance, Dr. Banks captures, conveys and helps us celebrate the heart of an amazing woman and Olympian, Coach Jarvis Scott. Congratulations Dr. Amanda Banks!

—Dr. James W. Dixon, II,
Pastor of The Community of Faith, Presiding Prelate and
Founder of Kingdom Builders Global Fellowship (KBGF),
Author, Social Justice Advocate

Amazing Race is a shining epitaph to the lifetime's work of Olympian Jarvis Scott in improving the lives of the numerous female athletes she coached.

The book reminds me in many ways of 'The Leadership Techniques of Attila the Hun' the best seller by Wess Roberts. But instead of a ruthless conqueror and his imagined interviewer we have a hardened Olympian who became an inspirational coach to generations of female athletes. One athlete in particular, the author Dr. Amanda Banks, had the sensitivity to realize that Coach J was also teaching her life lessons and that athletics competitions might be very similar to the future challenges she would face in her life.

Intrigued by this insight and armed with an inquisitive intelligence, Dr. Banks has listed these valuable lessons chapter by chapter. Sometimes they are amusing, more often harrowing in their tough love approach. Blessed with seemingly total recall of not only coach's words, but also her body language at the time, are brought vividly to life.

—Tony Duffy,
1968 Olympic Photographer,
Founder of Allsport Photography Agency

As a life-long learner, I am always looking for ways to be inspired so that I can strengthen and grow my own leadership skill set to motivate high performing teams. *Amazing Race* delivers 100% and is a beautiful tribute to Jarvis Scott and her ability to lead others by developing personal, trusting, and lasting relationships. She was teaching others about Servant Leadership before it was ever a "thing".

Whether your athletic status has deemed you a professional, amateur, occasional weekend warrior or if you are simply a spectator of life–you will be able to relate and appreciate the life lessons Coach Scott taught others to prepare them for future challenges life would certainly bring.

Dr. Amanda Banks, an athlete trained by the woman lovingly known as Jarvis, provides insight to a style of leadership intended to bring out the very best in a person. Each chapter is filled with examples of courage, resilience, perseverance, and the power of passion making this book a wonderful and worthwhile read that encourages self-reflection.

There is no doubt Jarvis Scott deeply touched the hearts of many and the valuable lessons she taught years ago are more relevant to emerging leaders than ever before.

—Dina Jeffries,
CEO, South Plains Food Bank

Amazing Race exemplifies the essence of Jarvis Scott's life. The chapters define how she overcame struggles and adversity to become a strong athlete, teammate, leader, coach, and friend. Her accomplishments and success were immeasurable on and off the track. *Amazing Race* includes life lessons Jarvis passed on to many athletes she coached over the years. I'm thankful to be one of the many athletes whose life she touched by coaching and mentoring.

—Sharon Moultrie-Bruner,
Head Track and Field Coach, South Grand Prairie High School,
Texas Tech University All-American (Long Jump), Texas Tech
University Hall of Fame (Long Jump)

AMAZING
RACE

AMAZING RACE

Inspiring Stories and Winning Leadership
Lessons from 1968 Olympian and Coach,

JARVIS SCOTT

AMANDA BANKS, PH.D.

I have tried to recreate events, locales and conversations from my memories of them. To protect privacy, in some instances I have changed the names of individuals and places, I may have changed some identifying characteristics and details such as physical properties, occupations and places of residence.

Stand Firm Publishing, LLC

www.getamazingrace.com

ISBN: 979-8-9856456-0-6 (Paperback)
ISBN: 979-8-9856456-1-3 (Ebook)

Photograph credits appear on page 231

Book Design: Authorsupport.com

Printed in the United States of America

For Mama

My hero, my hurricane.
Thank you for modeling resilience in the face of adversity
and loving others without limits.

♥

Table of Contents

Introduction

As the elevator ascended, I inhaled and let out a gasp that eclipsed the silence. And as the door slid open, thoughts of losing my coach consumed me. I thought I would chuck up lunch. Not like jitters prior to a race or the triple jump. I was doubled over at the thought of visiting the woman who coached many young athletes on how to win.

When I stepped out of the elevator, the pungent fumes of bleach antiseptic greeted me. My pace slowed as I walked into the hospital room. Overwhelmed, my emotions kicked to overdrive. I choked back the tears and took a deep breath. The nurse had just finished checking Coach Jarvis Scott's vitals.

Even though she was a former track and field Olympian and a world record holder, lifting a tennis ball for Coach Scott was impossible. I felt every lump in my throat.

The stethoscope halfway over her shoulder, the nurse asked, "Are you one of her athletes?"

Engulfed by gratitude, my eyes glossed over.

"Yes, one of many."

"I can tell she's a fighter," she said.

As the nurse left the room, I fixed my eyes on the wounded warrior. Her frail body lie in the hospital bed, but she gave me no sign. Coach Scott had no mobility. An ambush-style attack ravaged her body. Was she paralyzed? I sat at her bedside and reflected on the many times she told us not to give up. Uncertain if she could hear me, I spoke those same words right back into her spirit.

"There's a tiger in you, Coach Scott."

"You can do this."

"You're a fighter."

"Don't give up. ... Run past the finish."

I began calling out the names of former teammates and told her we were all praying for her recovery. Though I wanted a response, her ebony eyes remained anchored on some distant point. My chest and throat tightened as I looked for that coach's scan. She didn't blink. No nod. Not even a murmur.

The nurse entered the room. She shifted Coach Scott's body in her bed and said, "She's going to make it. Coach is a fighter."

As much as I fought it, my heart filled with sadness. I bent over, kissed Coach on the forehead, and whispered in her ear, "Your work is not complete."

Standing outside of her hospital room, I wrapped my arms

around myself and rested my hands on my shoulders. "Please don't leave us," I thought. When I reached the main lobby, I made my way to the chapel. Sadness soon turned to joy as I began to reflect on some of her lessons.

For instance, she taught us not to allow detours in life to distract us from our purpose. When faced with trials, she reminded us that obstacles are used as stepping-stones to cross over from failure to success. In the face of adversity, she would also remind us about faith and fortitude: "Faith is an asset. It puts fight in a person so that he or she develops a resistance to defeat. Obstacles no longer own a person. That is what keeps you going when you seem defeated."

Coach Scott taught us how to fight back in the presence of naysayers or enemies. Never one to place emphasis on the opinion others had of her, she'd say, "Don't empower your rivals with ammunition they don't have. You're the one with the edge." Jarvis learned the power of self-control at an early age. "Let your meekness be your strength. If I can do it, you can too."

Jarvis endured hardships. But she believed that your responses when navigating through life's tough moments could make the difference in being the victor or victim.

She strived to instill resilience and fortitude into anyone who had an ear to listen. The giant of a coach knew that her words had power to increase confidence and calm fears for those who would heed her positive messages and even her admonitions. More than standing on the podium to receive a medal, she wanted us to become a champion at the greatest sport called life.

Utilizing lessons from track and field would hopefully transfer to our everyday lives as we reached mile markers along life's interstate. More than developing great track and field athletes, Coach Scott yearned to train and strengthen our minds. By doing so, we could overcome internal struggles and learn to embrace adversity. She believed that cultivating a growth mind-set would build resilience, foster discipline, and unite women and men from different races, ethnicities, communities, and countries. Coach Scott wanted student-athletes to be relentless with not only setting goals but working toward the goals. The reminder to make every workout and every race count was a clarion call to make every moment matter. Leading others was Jarvis's life work, and the possibilities were limitless.

Who has inspired your life? For me, that person was Jarvis Scott, and her story will inspire you too.

What did she see in me? A naïve eighteen-year-old, I first stepped foot on the Texas Tech University campus in 1986, without ever seeing her face. A first-generation college student, I had no blueprint for navigating college. No recruiting visit, beautiful brochures, or other fanfare preceded my arrival.

I walked out of the Lubbock airport and into the red Chevette that awaited me. As we exited the airport, I realized the panoramic view of the awe-inspiring multi-hued mountains of El Paso that I knew would be replaced with cotton fields and flat plains.

New to the triple jump, and a mediocre sprinter, I stood five feet five and weighed 112 pounds. I wasn't the strongest, nor the fastest, but would leave Texas Tech University as an All-American and Southwest Conference Champion in the triple jump. More importantly, I left with a bachelor's degree. In 2005, I earned a PhD and was inducted into the Texas Tech Hall of Fame. In 2014, an induction into the Southwest Conference Hall of Fame filled my heart with humility and gratitude. While proud moments for me, none of it would be possible without Coach Jarvis Scott.

Because she never got a chance to write her book, I am writing it for her. Jarvis Scott's legacy is a testament to the infinite possibilities available to us when we overcome adversity. The aim of this book is to inspire, impact, and encourage you as you compare pieces of Coach Scott's life with your personal, spiritual, or professional life. The collection of stories, quotes, and anecdotes will fill your heart with life, love, sadness, and laughter.

Revolving around the central tenet that struggles, strain, and strife can still lead to success, each chapter will focus on different principles from stories in Jarvis's life that are applicable to your role as a leader. Reading this book will help improve your leadership abilities as you deal with life circumstances and challenges.

You will learn how events don't define you but can help others to achieve resilience. You will be inspired to not only reflect but to grow and learn as a leader.

Amid our racial climate and stressful times, the life and leadership of Coach Jarvis Scott will impact and influence your life as well as generations to come.

Jarvis's ability to bring others along was her greatest asset as a leader. Regardless of her struggles, she knew others would need the strength and resilience to face personal battles. Jarvis also recognized the importance of being connected to nature. "We are nature," she'd say. It was years before I realized her love for butterflies. There seemed to be an interconnection with Jarvis and the winged beauties.

What's so special about butterflies? Their uniqueness begins with the butterfly hatching eggs which become new caterpillars. The way a butterfly reinvents itself can provide us with lifelong lessons and answers as we face our own obstacles.

Developing into a leader mirrors the metamorphosis of a butterfly. The process is necessary for growth and success. Butterflies are symbols of a healthy surrounding. Their ability adapt to different climates and conditions makes them unique. When wet, the wings of a butterfly become heavy. To take flight, they sit and wait for the water to evaporate. That resilience symbolizes life and transformation.

The transformation process isn't easy, but by putting these principles into practice, you will become a stronger and a better leader. This book will give you strength for your own personal journey. You will find a recap of a leadership principle modeled by Coach Scott at the end of each chapter.

Do you want to achieve success? If so, the path begins with helping others succeed.

CHAPTER 1

The Call to Change Your Mind-Set

> *"Sure, I experienced a lot of racial prejudice. ... As a child, I had my first encounter with prejudice in Waco, Texas. I saw what people were talking about."—J*

Prepared by Prejudice

Hope soars when you chase your shadow. Skipping cracks on the sidewalk, beads of sweat trickled down her forehead. The inescapable heat during midsummers in Waco felt steamy. Fresh braided plaits bobbed and weaved like the heat off the street that created a mirage of an oasis of water. Little Jarvis's clothes became dampened with each stride. But it didn't matter. Summer tasted sugary, and the corner store's saltwater taffy and Slap Stix lollipop had already reached her palate.

1

Nearby, overgrown weeds invaded the park bench. Just as Jarvis darted across the street, a black vehicle came into sight.

The revving of the engine grew louder. Out of the corner of her eye, flashes of black loomed in on her. Panic surged through her heart but froze her feet. And before she understood the racial slurs being hurled, the front bumper collided with her. She flew into the air and rolled down a hill and into a ravine.

As she raised her head, the stink of the burning rubber filled her nostrils. The muck on her clothes plastered her body. As the car sped away, she whimpered, "I have dreams, I have dreams, I have dreams."

For a moment she blocked the pain, but her attempt to get up failed. To look at people running to her rescue made her veins and heart pound like a jackhammer. She mustered up the strength to pull herself out of the ravine. Though her knees buckled, she continued home. Rendered speechless, the bystanders stared in amazement, but she never noticed them.

Tattered clothes not only hung off her shoulders but the blood dripping from her knees covered the skin that now dangled. As the tears blurred her vision, she found strength in the figure that awaited her.

And now her voice grew louder. In the oldest grandchild's mind, the woman could box with God.

Young Jarvis bolted to the porch and jumped into her grandmother's arms. Her grandmother's voice trembled.

"They could have killed you!" she yelled.

The fragrance of her Avon perfume brought comfort.

"But they didn't," Jarvis said. Although the incident became the talk of the neighborhood, it also made little Jarvis more vigilant. She bounced back.

Unfortunately, later that summer, the black car reappeared. While strolling home from the store, two men and a woman tried to chitchat with Jarvis.

"Do you need a ride?" the woman asked. The blouse she wore screamed Marilyn Monroe, but the haircut told another story. More like June Cleaver. She took in the ring on the driver's hand as he thrummed his fingers on the door. His lips curved upside down.

"Hey there, niglet. A quarter is a lot of money for a little colored girl."

A flood of impending danger overtook Jarvis, and she took off running into a zigzag pattern all the way home. Now seeing the faces of the would-be kidnappers, her voice shrilled with sheer horror.

"Grandma!" she cried out.

The screen door flung open. Her grandmother's eyes widened as the car sped away. Her hands held Jarvis's head so close to her chest, the rapid beating of her grandmother's heart buzzed Jarvis's ears.

After wiping the tears from Jarvis's face, she began rubbing her back and said, "Thank you, Lord, for being a present help in time of trouble."

As I write this, I reflect on the first time I heard Jarvis talk about that attempted kidnapping. "Still I Rise" was the theme for the 2010 Black History Month program at Lyons Chapel Baptist Church in her honor. Standing behind the podium, she spoke about the harrowing experience that not only taught her to be alert but to master her mind-set. The strength in her story soon replaced the silence that hung in the air. Jarvis acknowledged the scary moment but also recognized the importance of refocusing on the positive. She also understood the power of words and guarded her tongue and thoughts.

> *"As a child, I remember living by a train track. All the houses were compact shotgun houses. There was not much room for furniture. Not even a bed. My parents had two mattresses for their bed. The kids slept on the floor with an assortment of blankets."—J (March 7, 2010)*

Prepared by Poverty

The birth of their baby girl unearthed a joy Mr. Ivory Sr. and Mrs. Johnnie Mae Scott had ever known. Jarvis LaVonne Scott graced the world on Resurrection Sunday, April 6, 1947, in Waco, Texas. Signs of poverty in the Scott home were apparent. Was it true? The poorer the people, the narrower the house? No hallways. Every room lined up in a row. From the front room, you could see out the back door. Not to mention, a clean exit for a bullet. But opening the front and back door became a sure way to let the fresh air circulate throughout the entire house.

Lunch and dinner sometimes included mayonnaise or syrup sandwiches, but the Scotts distracted the kids from focusing on their hunger. Relief came. World War II provided an economic opportunity for thousands of blacks willing to move westward. Ivory Scott secured a job in the aerospace industry.

Escaping drudgery soon placed Texas in the Scotts' rearview mirror. Motivated by the dream, the family packed their belongings and set out for California. Highways in Texas showed no trace of moisture, as the sun's wrath created a never-ending billow over the asphalt like a bed of coal. When the day ran into darkness, Jarvis slept on the floorboard of the car. And when she woke, they were more than six hundred miles away from home, in El Paso.

Some eight hours later, the family arrived in Phoenix. White smoke billowed from under the hood of their car. Out of options, the family sat in the scorching heat.

Like every other American, the Scotts wanted to travel without restraints. Sadly, a road atlas would not suffice, because Jim Crow existed as much in the west as in the south. Ivory Scott wanted to keep the family alive and prevent any mishaps or mistreatment. So, he would use a travel guide for black travelers. *The Green Book* listed the Winston Inn in Phoenix as one of a few Negro hotels but getting there posed a problem. Rather than risk the family's safety, he opted for the alternative. He watched his family as they slept in the car and waited for Uncle Tommy, who picked up the family in Phoenix and drove them to California.

Jarvis Lavonne Scott, born April 6, 1947 in Waco, Texas.

Easter Sunday, approximately 1950 in Waco, TX. From left: Ivory Scott, Jr., Ivory Scott, Sr., and Jarvis Scott

Precious memories; approximately 1950. From left: Ivory Scott, Jr., Ronald Scott, and Jarvis Scott

Stability in the arms of mother. Seated with mother, Johnnie Mae Scott, Ronald Scott and Jarvis Scott

Finding Her Voice

When the family arrived in Los Angeles, they moved into the Jordan Downs Projects. The recent construction comprised seven hundred units but clashed with the bright lights and palm trees that lined the rest of Los Angeles. Like the game Monopoly, the wealth gap of Boardwalk and Baltic Avenue came to life in Watts. No sun-kissed sands, shiny beaches, or majestic mountains.

Instead, toxic steel mills and factories surrounded the community. Signs of despair, danger, and dilapidation were all around Watts. Graffiti, price gouging, high unemployment, failing schools, teenage pregnancy, and poor transit systems were just some indications you were a special kind of broke. Health issues and no public hospital nearby exacerbated the problems. Outsiders viewed Watts as a death trap. For young Jarvis, walks home from her elementary school included witnessing violence, gangs, prostitution, drinking, and drugs.

How do you describe growing up in Watts? "Unimaginable," she said.

Despite her best efforts, painful memories stuck like pictures in an old photo album. She struggled to rid her mind of the sight of a police officer beating her brother over the head with a club.

Amid the division and strife, the burden and blessing fell on her parents to help their children make sense of it all. They filled days and evenings with news stories about the moon landing. It wouldn't be long before the six Scott children would also watch news stories about the civil rights movement. During that time, Jarvis found her voice.

While seated at the kitchen table, Jarvis was glued to her father as he shared personal stories. The army veteran risked his life overseas to fight Hitler's supremacy but returned home to battle inferior treatment and systemic racism. The door to home ownership slammed in his face when the G.I. Bill dismissed the sacrifice of black soldiers. White soldiers were matriculating on college and vocational school campuses, but black soldiers were denied enrollment or supplied subpar equipment. Jarvis's zeal for learning about the civil rights movement became apparent.

Her body stiffened reading about the "Mississippi Appendectomy" her hero, civil rights activist Fannie Lou Hamer, underwent without her approval. While Fannie Lou was under anesthesia to have a tumor removed from her uterus, a white doctor performed a hysterectomy.[1]

Jarvis's voice became brittle when she said, "I was fifteen years old when the police attacked and arrested her."

But she marveled at Fannie Lou's tenacity. The youngest of twenty children, and daughter of sharecroppers, Hamer refused to back down to white supremacy ideologies that prevented blacks from voting. She helped to organize voting rights drives across the state of Mississippi, cofounded the Freedom Democratic Party, and served as a field secretary for the Student Nonviolent Coordinating Committee (SNCC).[2] Regardless of the suffering she endured, Fannie Lou Hamer was known to have never muttered a harsh word toward her critics.

Just a few months later, Jarvis and her family sat in the living room and watched as nearly a quarter of a million people gathered near the Lincoln Memorial. As Dr. Martin Luther King Jr. stood at the podium, Jarvis locked on the educator and civil and women's rights activist Dorothy Height on the television screen. To the right of Dr. King and wearing a black-and-white hat and black suit, the president of the National Council of Negro Women looked on. Jarvis longed for a strong presence of black women at the podium.

"To be black and a woman in America is the hardest job. The men missed an opportunity to honor the voice and contributions of the black women in the movement," she said.

Still, the Scott family and the marchers were uplifted. Sunrise at the Santa Monica Pier was no comparison to the radiant smiles in the Scott home that August.

But less than thirty days later, the pitch of her mother's wail silenced the house. A bomb at the 16th Street Baptist Church killed four black girls and seriously injured another in Birmingham, Alabama, as they sat in Sunday school. Jarvis gagged. The room spun as she embraced her mother.

"Mama ..."

Even if comforting her mother helped, she didn't know what to say. The safest and most sacred place had become susceptible to the worst type of harm because some whites hated blacks.

Would young Jarvis become fearful or fervent in her faith? Would she fight, or would she flee?

Recalling those times, the trills and turns of the Queen of Gospel, Mahalia Jackson, drifted from the CD player like the archangel had descended from heaven. It took Jarvis back to that September. And now her eyes glossed over. She sighed.

"The lives of innocent children meant nothing," she said.

Would history shape her behavior?

"I didn't know what to do. But I was determined to make a difference," she said.

Jarvis continued to study the civil rights movement and the lives of civil rights activists.

"Life in the projects was fragile," she said. "I was faced with making decisions that would impact my life."

No matter the daily trials, Jarvis clung to the vision orated by Dr. Martin Luther King Jr. on August 28, 1963.

"That 'I Have a Dream' speech stuck with me. I knew I could become anything I wanted," she said. "What, where, and when I didn't know. But I leaned on my faith and learned how to fight fair."

More importantly, Jarvis started the journey to discover her authentic self. She let go of any desire to conform, and instead found the courage to be herself. She critically examined her beliefs and values and made sure they aligned with her goals and passion. Speaking up and expressing herself regardless of who approved or disapproved became a part of her choice to be vulnerable. But Jarvis realized that a part of that vulnerability had to include providing opportunities for others to also express themselves. And despite the chaos and racial unrest, Jarvis came to realize that to see change in society meant finding meaningful ways to contribute to humanity.

She took control of her thoughts and emotions. The same can go for you.

Having been taught by Jarvis, I took control of my thoughts and emotions and learned not to react so quickly to negative situations. While it wasn't an overnight process, I had to learn to recognize my triggers. Once I recognized my triggers, instead of suppressing what I felt, I began to express whatever emotion I felt. Once I named the emotion, I assessed and analyzed my thoughts. And when my belief was negative, I learned to reframe my thinking.

Do you want to change your mind-set and develop the personal power Jarvis had? Pay attention to your circumstances. Whether you have assurance or anxiety in the face of adversity, your mind believes what your mouth says. So it is especially important that you pay attention to your words. If you are not careful, like old habits, the irrational beliefs will build up. Like Jarvis, learn to guard your mind and your mouth.

Mind-set is everything. The way you interpret your personal experiences and environment is directly related to your behavior. Essentially, your brain is reprogrammed, and you begin to learn new ways of thinking and doing. Mastering your mind-set takes a lot of focus and fortitude but is worth the work.

Jarvis's routine began with training her brain. Early on, she began engaging in self-talk. And later she started journaling and writing affirmations. Regardless of her background and personal encounters, she did not allow negative thinking to clutter her mind. And instead of fixating on her present condition, she focused on her long-term goals.

Leadership Principle #1

Great leaders do not allow circumstances to limit their beliefs about themselves or those around them. Since you can't always predict difficulties, what you can do is pivot. Don't panic. Your training will pay off. That is, if you are willing to adapt and learn new language. The moment you decide to make the shift, you will see how the mind is a powerful source. Are you ready to plug in?

CHAPTER 2

The Call to Respond and Not React

> "*The race riots took shape. The attacks, the fires, destruction, and looting. People just went crazy. The police did nothing. They let people do what they wanted.*"—J

Burn, Baby, Burn

Despite passage of the Civil Rights Act of 1957, it would not change the landscape for blacks in America. The 1960s was marked with racial segregation, racial disparities in schools and the workplace, voting rights struggles, political strife, and antiwar sentiment. Systemic policies and practices that projected poor outcomes for the urban community signaled a dream deferred. Watts residents grew embittered at the conditions that created two divergent Americas.

When the California Highway Patrol pulled over twenty-one-year-old black motorist Marquette Frye, and his brother, on Avalon Boulevard and 116th Street, bystanders perceived the traffic stop as another case of driving while black. As dissension brewed, the crowd and police backup swelled. What began with hollering and cussing escalated into physical altercations.[3]

Six days in August, in 1965, a veil of dark clouds descended upon the souls of blacks, mushrooms of toxic smoke replacing the blue metropolis skies. Fire engulfed buildings; cars were burned and destroyed; businesses looted; blood was shed.

Marching through the streets with semiautomatic weapons and pistols in obvious sight, no place hid the sound of sirens as thousands of law enforcement and National Guardsmen populated Watts.

"Please go in your homes! Please go in your homes! This area is being closed. Please go in your homes!" the Guardsmen demanded over the bullhorn.[4] They banged on the door of every tenant in the Jordan Downs Projects and asked how many black males were in the home.

"My mom told them six," Jarvis said.

In the wake of the riots, Jarvis became familiar with the scene walking along 102nd Street. Excitement surged as people, in complete daylight, carried off items they considered free: furniture, clothing, liquor, televisions, items not bolted to the ground. Police handcuffed black men of different ages.

Onlookers heard the dispatcher over the radio: "All units. Looters at Sixty-two and Broadway. All units, looters at Sixty-two and Broadway."[5]

While the looting angered Jarvis, she understood the reaction. She likened the mind-sets of most to what Dr. Martin Luther King Jr. stated: "Rioting is the voice of the unheard." Jarvis believed that the plight of Watts residents fell on deaf ears of the United States government. Conditions such as high illiteracy rates, high unemployment rates, and failing schools were not condemned. That same sentiment was also shared by civil rights activist Bayard Rustin, who joined Dr. King in Watts to meet with the mayor, police chief, and other public officials days after the riots.

"I think the real cause is that Negro youth—jobless, hopeless— does not feel a part of American society. ... People who feel a part of the structure do not attack it," Rustin said.[6]

Signs of despair and dilapidation were all around. A year before the riots, Proposition 14 reversed the 1964 Rumford Act, prohibiting racial discrimination in housing.[7] To make matters worse, health issues were also a concern as there was no public hospital within eight miles. Watts also had one of the country's worst public transit systems. General Motors, a big employer in the area, was approximately twenty-two miles away from Watts. Unless you were fortunate to own a car, a one-way trip on the bus took four hours and forty-five minutes.[8] Consequently, Watts became fertile ground for a riot, or what residents deemed their "Manifesto."

Watts turned into a war zone, as sounds of snipers' rifles cracked throughout the day. Night mirrored fireworks on the 4th of July.

Residents walking the streets of Watts faced more devastating ruin. Amidst the chaos, eighteen-year-old Jarvis headed home from Jordan High School, where she worked as a typist. An inferno rose in her mind watching a looter come out of the dry cleaners with her family members' clothing items.

"Hey!"

The looter fled, but Jarvis broke out in a sprint after the thief! She caught up to the young brother, shoved him, and snatched the clothes from his arms.

As she cut across the street, the unrest continued to ignite. Rioters overturned some cars and burned others, also looting stores, and firemen doused the flames of burning buildings.

Los Angeles police were as much heard as seen. The white LAPD officer demanded, "Get your hands up high! You can lift them higher than that. ... The first one to drop their hands is a dead man!"

As Jarvis watched the scene on television, the white officer exercised no mercy on black women. "Get your hands up! Get 'em up high over your head!" the officer warned.

The crowd lashed out as they watched the officer slam a young teen to the ground. "Kill the white man!" someone in the crowd yelled about the police officer.

Racial harmony vanished and residents reached their tipping point. Tired of being sick and tired, resentment and pandemonium erupted in the inner city.

Trash and smoldering ashes covered many parts of the ghetto community. Over one hundred square blocks of the city were in ruin.

"I couldn't put a price tag on the damage," she said.

The rioting resulted in thirty-four deaths and more than one thousand injuries. Total damages cost over $40 million.[9]

Struggling with the aftermath, Jarvis worked hard to purge her mind of the seeds of destruction that transformed Watts into a cataclysmic abyss.

"I looked for a sign that my eyes were betraying me," she said. Seeing no sign, she began a process to work through her sadness and anger. "Our forefathers' hard work burned to the ground, and the LAPD did nothing to stop it," she said.

Overwhelming sorrow struck Jarvis as she read and listened to the media coverage of the riots. She sought to comprehend the "Us vs. Them" sentiment prevalent in newspapers and news outlets. Echoes of "Burn, baby, burn!" "Honkey," "Monkeys," "Hoodlums," and "Lawlessness" rang in her head.

"They talked about the effects but ignored the root cause of the riots. Where was the humanity? Why the failure to hear?" she asked.

Jarvis equated the response to watching the destruction from an ivory tower while closing an eye to the dark reality that plagued the inner city. While the media focused on the lawlessness, looting, and lament for material loss, they failed to mention the looting of property from redlining and housing discrimination. Nor was there any mention of a system that perpetuated mistrust of the police, low graduation rates, and high unemployment.

Because of her belief about the underlying causes of the rioting and looting, Jarvis longed for a change in the narrative of "we're on the top, they're on the bottom." She longed to hear stories about the lived experiences of residents who spent many hours riding on public transit to get to a low-paying job. Stories of students who attended failing schools. Stories of grocery store owners preying on welfare recipients by hiking up prices once they knew residents received their government checks. She prayed for the media to cover stories from a lens of equity and racial consciousness, stories that restored harmony and cultivated the frailty of our humanity.

Despite biased framing and slanted coverage, Jarvis's reasoning trumped rage. She decided that if she named her emotions, she could manage her reactions and respond in a manner that would tame the force of an angry current.

Businesses destroyed and dreams devastated during the 1965 Watts Riots.

Aerial view of a section of Watts during the 1965 riots.

Demonstrators surround a police car in Watts, Los Angeles (August 12, 1965)

"I had many more experiences with racial comments, but each one made me tougher, and made me who I am."—J

You Don't Belong Here

While playing in pickup baseball games in Alhambra, California, Jarvis felt a sense of belonging. No coaches and umpires—just kids at play. Excitement lingered on this Saturday afternoon because her team, the Dodgers, were coming off a win. Third in the lineup, with the first two reaching base, Jarvis stood at home plate. A natural, she swung with an explosion like the force of pulling back the string of a bow and arrow. Her skinny legs helped propel the swing. Crack! Off to left field, the ball hung in midair and then bounced off the fence. Off in the distance, you could hear, "It is goooood!!" The adolescent boy tried to mimic the great Los Angeles Dodgers sportscaster, Vin Scully. Two runs scored, and Jarvis made it to third base.

Later in the game, while playing in the outfield, she caught a fly ball. A young teenaged white girl on the opposing team yelled at Jarvis.

"Tar Baby!"

If only the insult stuck with the comeback kid.

Hell-bent on agitating the maverick, she told the others on her team, "Don't let Jarvis spook you!" She learned to view her whiteness as invisible.

To the teenaged girl's dismay, Jarvis did not react with anger. Instead, she channeled her energy into the task at hand and handled her next two chances to retire the batters. The incident marked one of many where she learned to respond and not react.

Another incident occurred when Jarvis was in her early twenties, after qualifying for a USA track team. Housed at UCLA,

Jarvis sat in on a team meeting when out of nowhere, the insult rang out from a fellow competitor: "Black people are lazy! They won't get off their butts and work. All they do is take, take, take!"

How dare he spew such vomit! A flicker of irritation arose. However, the urge to resist anger overruled. Instead, Jarvis sashayed across the room and leaned into her white male counterpart sitting in the chair, her nose brushing against his cheek.

"Am I?" she thought.

She laid one on his lips.

He sprang to his feet as though every stereotype had been sucked out of him. A group of giggles and gasps followed as he burst out the door.

Jarvis's response got everyone's attention. It became her way of belting out the message from a citizen of Watts that never escaped her memory: "Look at me! Look at me! Know me for what I am! Look at me if you can!"

It vividly called to mind watching firsthand how Jarvis had learned to respond versus react when I was on her track team at Texas Tech University. Because of the shilly-shally weather in West Texas, the women's track team looked forward to Tempe's year-round sunshine when we went for a track meet. Upon our return to Lubbock, the polar night had unleashed confetti of hominy. Safety came first for Coach Scott. Tapping on the steering wheel, she surveyed the parking lot and pulled up on the driveway reserved for official Texas Tech vehicles.

As a result, the police pulled up behind the van. Flashes of blue and red lit up Gaston Residence Hall matching a Christmas display. The sound of ice crunching under his boots loomed around outside as the officer approached the van. Silence eclipsed the van.

"I pulled you over because you cannot park here."

Suddenly, Coach Scott's expression dulled.

"I need to see your license."

"Sure."

"Is this your address? Do you still live on 25th Street?"

While handing the officer her license, Jarvis sucked in a breath, exhaled, and then responded. "Yes, that's my address. And I will not let my girls walk from the parking lot in the snow with luggage," she said.

"I need you to step out of the vehicle," he said.

Silence. Our blood boiled.

But a few minutes passed ... and he left without issuing a ticket.

Jarvis viewed her response as one that was logical. She knew that reacting would only lead to a verbal sparring, at the very least. At best, by responding, she and the officer could engage in a healthy dialogue. But mastering your mind-set has no endpoint.

Later that spring Coach Scott and I chatted as we walked toward the athletic offices at the south end of Jones Stadium. A third reflection came into sight as we approached the double glass doors.

"What are you doing? You don't belong here," he said.

Angered by the police officer's expression, I clenched my jaw. I had not yet learned Coach Scott's lesson of responding and not reacting. She showed me another way. She never flinched.

No break in her stride, she continued toward the front door. Her hand glided out of her pocket so smooth. I couldn't hear the jingle if I wanted. She placed the key in the passage. Every click as she turned the key sounded as if in Dolby Cinema.

"I belong here, and I am not going anywhere!"

The officer hesitated and then took a step toward Coach Scott.

"Well, I guess you do belong here."

The words spat out of his mouth. His eyes looked as angry as a raging fire because of his own snap judgment.

A smile emerged ... or did she smile? No signs of a smile line or a spark in her eyes appeared. In an instant, the white officer's tone retriggered memories of police confrontations while growing up in Watts.

Her posture relaxed. And placing her hand on the doorknob, Coach Scott opened her office door. He mumbled, "Have a good evening."

As I reflected on my years competing at Texas Tech, police

encounters with Jarvis were unforgettable. I wondered why she didn't let the officer have it.

Coach Scott endured the experiences that I, and others, deemed as prejudicial treatment. Former hurdler Aimee Frescaz-Kraenzel said, "We were all so young, but observant. We understood the university wasn't good to her."

Like Aimee, I struggled with the mistreatment. Where was the anger? For Jarvis, becoming a conduit of growth for student-athletes carried more weight than getting out of character.

And now an adult, I searched for the right words. We sat in her living room on January 9, 2012.

"How did you do it?"

In a calm and unhurried voice, she said, "Resistance is inevitable. You must learn to respond and not react."

Few, but profound, words. I waited for her to say something else. Nothing.

The humming of the space heater filled the room. And then, "At some point, you will experience headwinds. Decide how you will get through it. Because it will come," she said.

In the face of opposition, managing your emotions is an important skill of leadership. Mark Twain wrote, "Anger is an acid that can do more harm to the vessel in which it is stored than to anything on which it is poured."

Anger is a normal emotion. There is nothing wrong with getting angry. It's what you do with your anger. You can respond or you can react. Responses are more thoughtful and deliberate, whereas reactions are more knee-jerk and impulsive.

Team photo for 1971 Pan American Games held in Cali, Colombia.

Leadership Principle #2

Great leaders learn to manage their emotions because they recognize that reacting will lead to frustration, fatigue, and failure. They meet the opposition face-to-face while remaining focused on the task at hand. Great leaders also see opposition for what it is. A deterrent and distraction. Instead of yielding to the resistance, great leaders respond by not compromising their values. They are firm without adding fuel to the fire. Instead, great leaders capitalize by exposing untruths.

Responding is a life skill. With preparation and practice, you too can learn to express yourself in a manner that is meek, rather than weak. By choosing not to react you are modeling self-control. There will certainly be situations and events that push your buttons. But the choice will always be yours. Are you up for the challenge?

CHAPTER 3

The Call to Push and Pull

> *"We faced tough life decisions, but I knew I could become anything I wanted. The good or ugly. The neighborhood didn't offer opportunities for you to advance, so we worked even harder to make our mark. I had no playbook for success but wanted to leave a lasting legacy. What, where, and when, I wasn't certain, but I focused on possibilities."—J*

No Place Else to Go

Since there were no interscholastic athletics for girls at Jarvis's high school, the Presidential Physical Fitness Test marked Jarvis's rite of passage. The eighteen-year-old senior whizzed through pull-ups, sit-ups, push-ups, and one-mile run.

Dim lighting crept through the narrow hallway. As Jarvis hurried to math class, her name echoed through the hall.

"What does he want?" she mumbled.

When she turned around, the principal motioned her toward him. Speaking in a commanding voice, he said, "Come to my office."

Before she took a seat, the recruiting spiel started. "Have you ever run track?"

Without ever acknowledging her "No, sir," he told Jarvis about Fred T. Jones's campus visit the following day.

Fred T. Jones possessed an eye for true grit. As a result, in Jarvis, he saw a tough young lady with an uncanny ability to focus and fight.

"Negativity does not discourage you. Give this a try."

It didn't take long for the high schooler to join the Los Angeles Mercurettes. Training with a club team at West Los Angeles College replaced racing in the middle of the street against the neighborhood kids. Jarvis adapted to a different routine. The burn in her hamstrings and buttocks compared to no other. Before long, Jarvis's muscles bulged. Like a goddess out of the Nile, her chocolate lean legs sculpted her frame.

With the physical transformation came a mental shift. First, Jarvis accepted responsibility for the terrific, the terrible, and tolerable in her life. But she refused to make excuses, as they only lead to stagnation. Instead, Jarvis focused on changing her outcome. So what if she lived in Watts. The foot of oppression heavy on their necks would not be a stumbling block.

As the days and weeks passed, her insight into the sport of track and field increased. While there were tough days, the support she received from her school, family, and friends made everything worthwhile.

Quitting was not an option.

"Believe me, it was hard! It was tough to stay motivated to reach the success that everyone believed I could reach," she said.

"That dream of making a mark in track, along with meeting and competing with those athletes I saw competing in the Olympics, was soon a reality. I began traveling around the world, learning unique cultures and lifestyles. It was fulfilling."

Jarvis adapted a "whatever it takes" mentality. And dreams of escaping the ghetto ignited her determination to persevere. Jarvis decided to create her own success story. As much as she was persistent, she demonstrated patience.

"I experienced hurting and pain firsthand and trained for almost four years, from 6:00 a.m. until 9:00 a.m. and 6:00 p.m. until 9:00 p.m.," said Jarvis, known as Jaye to teammates.

Wow! Shaking her head, Jaye's teammate and roommate, Barb Ferrell, said, "I'd get to the track and Jaye would be running. When I left the track, she would still be running. I just sat and waited."

Jarvis didn't have much time to squeeze in extracurricular activities. So, when practice ended, she headed for the University of Southern California Religious Center, where she worked as a secretary. The days and nights ran into one another. Her muscles fatigued and eyes burned from sleep deprivation.

"Even though there were times I couldn't go another step, my coach told me every day to keep going," she said. "People asked me why? I wanted the result. Besides, there was no place else to go."

Jarvis also wanted the best outcome for others. As a coach she was relentless in her pursuit with helping others to achieve success. The following anecdote is an example.

For long distance runner Red Cloud, a Jicarilla Apache, a track scholarship to run for Texas Tech Men's Track and Field and Cross Country team provided an escape from the ghetto. While Jarvis made it out of Watts, Red Cloud survived Five Points in Denver, where he also encountered racial tensions, police brutality, and gangs. His father died when he was ten years old.

Red Cloud admired and respected Jarvis for overcoming her personal struggles and achieving athletic accomplishments. He also recognized that Jarvis's struggles didn't harden her heart nor did her Olympic accomplishments inflate her ego.

Long distance runner Maria Medina didn't know much about Jarvis's personal struggles but knew of her Olympic accomplishments. Maria wanted results and believed that Jarvis could help.

It was April 24, 1981. The high school senior out of Bel Air High School in El Paso, Texas, had just finished running the 3200 meters at the regional track meet in Lubbock, Texas. Surprised to hear that Coach Scott had left the meet, Maria took off after her.

As she exited the gate, Maria yelled out, "Coach Scott!" Making her way to Coach Scott, she extended her hand and said, "Hi, I'm Maria Medina. Nice to meet you. Did you see my race?"

"Yes, I saw your race," Coach Scott replied.

Her quizzical smile may have left Maria uncertain, but Coach Scott knew she had found a winner and offered Maria a scholarship.

It wasn't the race alone but Maria's firm hand grip and persistence to catch up to Jarvis.

Maria and Red Cloud bonded quickly. Red Cloud did not earn an e-z pass to hang around Maria. Regardless of the commonalities he and Coach Scott shared, she remained mindful and on guard of the company her girls kept.

But after passing Coach Scott's clearance test, he became a fixture with the women's program. He assisted Coach Scott with driving the van to track meets and ran early morning workouts with the team.

"You can say I was her assistant," he said.

It wasn't long before Red Cloud and Maria became students of the push and pull principle.

Morning workouts soon turned into morning and afternoon. Red Cloud's eyes danced at the opportunity to train with Coach Scott.

"How can I be the best?"

"You want to be the best? Jog six miles on the track," Jarvis said. "For every 400, I want you to sprint the last 100. Your mile should be under five minutes."

After fourteen laps, Red Cloud walked over to Jarvis. "That's not jogging. I can't do that."

"Then don't do it. Because if you don't think you can, you won't," Jarvis said.

Red Cloud's words and actions changed.

Maria had to learn to do the same. Jarvis never posted a workout. On any given day, the workout could be thirty-five 200-meter runs. Runners ran half of a full lap around the track. When finished, they walked across the field and ran another 200.

"How many left?" Maria asked.

Coach never raised her head from the clipboard. "When you finish," she said. The second and last time she told Maria, "When you beat the guys."

Head men's track coach Corky Oglesby would needle Red Cloud about training with the women's team: "If you train with girls, you will run like a girl," he said.

But Red Cloud welcomed being the punchline from teammates at track meets.

"Are you gonna run like a girl today?"

Red Cloud didn't make a fuss. "Yes! I am gonna run like a girl."

He ruled the track and lapped his teammates.

Soon, the guys began lining up to train with Jarvis. "We had one of the best teams because of her," Red Cloud said. "She gave us the proper tools to be a winner."

Maria Medina and Red Cloud

Strong finish in the 10K from Red Cloud at the Texas Tech Invitational (1984)

Eyes front, head high to the finish. Maria Medina at the Texas Tech Cross Country Invitational

Stay in the Boat

The 1981–1982 cross country and track season ended on a dismal note for Maria. After a poor showing at the Southwest Conference Outdoor Championships, Maria learned her scholarship would be cut.

Coach Scott and Maria's father were eerily similar about their advice.

"What are you going to do? Either get better or we will go get your things," her father told Maria.

Maria chose the first, and Coach Scott helped her out. In training runs, Jarvis ran ahead of the pack to set the pace and ensure that the runners ran a fast time. When she wasn't running on the track, she ran from one side of the track to the other during Maria's workouts. Before you knew it, she was implementing tactics to help runners withstand the elements that occurred during a competition.

Red Cloud was the perfect instigator: "Elbow her!" "Cut her off!" "Push her!" "Slow down!"

The strategy was unpredictable, but whatever Red Cloud did, Maria responded. She worked hard to run stride for stride with Red Cloud.

The tactics worked because there were some workouts when Red Cloud could no longer keep up with Maria. More importantly, she became the Southwest Conference Champion in the

1500 meters. In the fall of 1983, Maria competed at the NCAA Division I Cross Country Meet and placed sixty-seventh. "I never wanted to disappoint her," Maria said.

When pregnant and in her third trimester, Coach Scott had not traveled to the meet. When Jarvis received the meet results, she pumped her fists. Unfortunately, the request to reinstate Maria's scholarship midsemester was denied.

November 19, 1984, proved different, as Coach Scott accompanied Maria on a blistery fall day at University Park, Pennsylvania, for the NCAA Division I Cross Country Championship Meet. The race tactic: the pace was blazing.

"It never let up!" Maria said.

Despite the frigid temperature, the time at the one-mile mark was a splendid four minutes and fifty-four seconds! Just as she had always done, Coach Scott ran to specific spots in the race. The strategy worked, as Maria left the Keystone State with All-American honors.

Jarvis's methods weren't always welcomed.

"I will get it out of you today. You will bring out your guts!" she warned 400-meter runner Yvette Patterson, who longed for a break from Jarvis running with her. "Don't let me catch you," Jarvis, six months pregnant, said as she shot up the hill to catch Yvette.

"Jarvis! Cool it!" came the warning by Assistant Coach Beale

Tolbert, but it went unnoticed because limitations did not exist for Coach Scott.

Although Jarvis didn't catch Yvette, the quarter-miler wanted to punch a wall. She finished lifting weights and walked into Coach's office.

"I'm not doing this anymore. I quit."

"OK. I will call your parents to tell them not to send you a bus ticket. Now figure it out."

"You are so mean," Yvette said.

"You pranced in my office with a nasty attitude."

Yvette gritted her teeth.

"Now you have a choice. Door number one: I will see you in the morning for a workout. Door number two: Quit. You choose," Coach Scott said.

Years later while sitting in the living room, we laughed at the stories. And then Jarvis said, "Sailing will not always be easy, but you have to know when to push and know when to pull." I smiled and shook my head.

Still today, I ponder Jarvis's encouragement: "Stay in the boat." I don't know about you, but I've had moments in my life when I've needed a reminder to not jump ship. Those moments when the storm arises and the waves start crashing. Aside from the flash of forked lightning, darkness has enveloped me. The turbulence causes cold water to collide with my face and body, leaving me drenched and gasping for air. While at some point I might have panicked, I had to remind myself the life preserver was already on board. So whatever it looks like or feels like, don't abandon ship! As I encourage myself, let me encourage you too. You might be drenched, but you won't drown.

Focused on the finish at the Texas Tech Invitational Track Meet

Ready to race at the 1984 NCAA Division I Cross Country Championships in University Park, Pennsylvania

Yvette Patterson anchors the mile relay at the SWC Track and Field Championships

Leadership Principle #3

Great leaders model what they want from the team. For Jarvis, it was her willingness to participate in the workouts that pushed and pulled student-athletes. She was either running on the track, alongside the track, or across the cross country course. And when she was not running, she stayed engaged. Regardless of her position on the track, she did not allow outside elements to distract her. Instead, she took notice of every move her student-athletes made and verbally acknowledged when we did things well.

A leader's gift to deal with high pressure situations inspires their team members to bring their "A" game every day. Not only that, but in the middle of chaos or high pressure situations, team members will respond in a calm and collective manner. Leaders also make sure that members on the team share in the same vision.

The ability to provide unique and challenging opportunities for team members to grow is also a mark of a great leader. They recognize that what works for one may not work for another. They take the time to understand the strengths and limitations of their team and meet team members where they are. When leaders understand what makes each member tick, they push them beyond that space of complacency. Once team members know their leaders have their back, they are more likely to put in the work and be willing to go the extra mile.

As you work to push your team to its limit, make sure your pressure is purpose-driven. But keep in mind, some stretching is required.

CHAPTER 4

The Call to Keep Good Company

"Although you may not realize it, the impression you make on others is both favorable and lasting. A genuine friendship can benefit you in unexpected ways."—J

Through Thick and Thin

A short sprinter (100-meter, 200-meter, and long jump), Barb, hailed from Chicago and ran for the Chicago Zephyrs Track Club. The top teams in the country were the Tennessee Tigerbelles and the L.A. Mercurettes. Barb's coach, the great Jane Bernard Dickens, introduced the family to Fred T. Jones. Next, Barb's parents bought her a one-way ticket to Los Angeles.

Jarvis and Barb hit it off immediately. Becoming two of the first to run for the L.A. Mercurettes Track Club, they also became roommates and sister friends. Brutal workouts, coupled with a domineering coach, proved to be challenging, but Jarvis and Barb entertained themselves.

"We snuck out all the time. We climbed walls, trees, and poles. Whatever it took, we did it!" Barb said.

Who blamed them? Like Lou Gossett Jr.'s character in the movie *An Officer and a Gentleman*, Coach Jones remained in Marine Gunnery Sergeant Emil Foley mode and put his athletes through hell! Coaches and athletes struggled with Jones's system because athletes in his regime did not have much freedom. He scrutinized every area of their lives, including discouraging the girls from dating, wearing makeup, and talking to athletes from other teams.

Jarvis and Barb also had a male training partner, Reynaldo Brown. A Compton native, Reynaldo held the National High School record in the high jump. Because Coach Jones was impressed with his agility and flexibility, he asked Reynaldo to share stretching techniques with the Mercurettes.

A budding friendship between Reynaldo and Jarvis flourished. Surprisingly, Coach Jones approved of Reynaldo hanging around "his girls." Even still, the high schooler understood the implications of Jones's request for help.

"Coach didn't want guys coming around his girls because he thought they distracted the girls," Reynaldo said.

Yet, young brothers showed up to the track.

Skin complexions of the Nubian goddesses, ranging from caramel to dark chocolate, donned the track field. A triple threat, physiques of goddesses and personalities matched the skin tones. Neither the rules nor the chorus of expletives that flew out of Coach Jones's mouth hindered the fellas.

Regardless of the environment, Jarvis's focus on the track was impeccable. Every workout, every track meet, every day, she gave more than a 100 percent effort. Reynaldo watched the lean machine during practice.

"No matter what Coach had her do, she just did it. If she didn't understand, she'd ask questions. Jaye never complained and stayed committed," he said.

Yet, Barb and Jaye lived for free weekends. Capture a glimpse: music playing in the distance created a party atmosphere. Barb and Jaye turned the space in between their twin beds into a dance floor. Hips swayed, and fingers snapped to the beat.

Barb began singing "Stop! In the Name of Love," by The Supremes. Her fisted hand mirrored a microphone.

Jarvis joined in.

The two giggled and then sang the chorus together.

Excitement built for Barb. A date and a Gladys Knight review made sneaking out worth the risk.

Barb stepped outside for some fresh air during that intermission. And before reaching the curb, Coach Jones's 1965 white

Mustang appeared. Rendered speechless, her mouth hung open. Placing her hand over her mouth, Barb jumped back to the side of the building.

As she peeked around the corner, the parking lights illuminated like high beams on a dark deserted road. The shine of the full moon caused the silhouette of Coach Jones's big Jackson 5 Afro to appear even bigger. Barb could feel the tension. She didn't have to see his face to feel the anger.

Barb ran into a hallway across the street and laid low. She saw his car going back and forth. Ten minutes passed. Once darkness loomed, Barb made a dash and sprinted home.

Back home, she and Jaye devised a plan to thwart any repercussions from Coach Jones. Barb hurried to change out of her halter and bell-bottoms. She tossed her platform shoes into the closet, and the two put rollers in Barb's hair.

Sure enough, there was Coach Jones. As he entered the hallway, the female house monitor was the first person to greet him.

"Where's Barb?!"

His penetrating stare made her hands sweat.

She took Coach Jones upstairs to the room.

Every footstep echoed in the hallway, each thump ringing out like an air-raid siren. Clothed but with pink rollers affixed in place, Barb scurried into bed. As though running a race, she tried to control and slow her breathing. She closed her eyes. Seconds later,

Coach Jones was standing at her bedside. His narrow eyes clouded over as he looked at the pink sponge rollers decorating Barb's head. With a scowl on his face, Coach Jones checked his watch, turned, and exited the room.

The authoritative coaching style of Fred T. Jones never stopped Barb and Jarvis. One night the roomies went to a basketball game, and then to a party in Watts in the gym at Jordan High School.

As they entered the gym, the sounds of "I Heard it Through the Grapevine" by Gladys Knight and the Pips played. Otis Redding's "Try a Little Tenderness" and Aretha Franklin's "Respect" followed. Young soul brothers and soul sisters rocked platform shoes, corduroy suits, minidresses, bell-bottoms, and dashikis. They flooded the dance floor, dancing the shimmy, the twist, and the Watusi.

Two hours passed. Barb went to the ladies' room. She washed her hands and began powdering her face. The slamming of the door swinging open made her jump.

"Take off your shoes," Jarvis said.

"What?!" Barb said.

Jaye insisted. "Take off your shoes. They are about to fight!"

Before Barb's bare heels touched the ground, she heard pop, pop, pop, pop!! The sound of the bullets, people screaming, and feet trampling, frightened Jaye and Barb. With no effort, both runners bolted out of the window! And just like that, their first race together began with a bang!

While Jaye and Barb had a blast together, they worked hard to complete their job on the track. They also worked hard to cultivate their connection with one another. Jarvis and Barb spoke life into one another. They did so by encouraging one another to reach their goals. This included celebrating wins and lifting each other during losses. And while Jarvis and Barb valued each other's opinion, they were careful to listen and not judge.

Coach Fred T. Jones, founder of the Los Angeles Mercurettes

Jarvis and Barb, enjoying the sites of Mexico City (1968)

Reynaldo Brown, 1968 Olympic team photo. Reaching for higher heights

> *"We never know whose path we may cross. Through friendships we learn and teach. I am grateful for the joy of friendship."* —J

Beyond Black and White

Coach Fred T. Jones struggled to build warm and fuzzy relationships. Instead, he trained his athletes as though preparing for a battle. This was no secret to anyone, as the following anecdote shows.

The 1965 indoor track season was underway, and teams from across the country traveled to Albuquerque for the indoor meet.

Down the narrow hallway, Madeline Manning saw the team clustered in a huddle. The green and gold was the first clue they were Jones's team. Madeline competed for the Tennessee Tigerbelles, coached by Ed Templeton. They were also the top team in the country.

Madeline walked over to Barb. "Where are the 400- and 800-meter runners?" She did not see Jarvis sitting nearby.

Barb pointed her hand in Jarvis's direction. "She is sitting right here," she said. Jarvis glanced at Madeline and smirked.

"She was looking at me kind of funny, but spoke," Madeline said. The Tigerbelle from Tennessee State took two steps and locked eyes with Jarvis. "Great to meet you. I've heard so many wonderful things about you," Madeline said.

Jaye rose to her feet and extended her hand. "Hi, I'm Jarvis Scott. I run the 400, and sometimes the 800." The handshake signified a budding friendship instead of a rivalry.

As Madeline turned to leave, Coach Jones walked up.

"Hi, Coach Jones," Madeline said. With a distant look, he responded, "Hello, Madeline," he said with a soft growl.

There was no difficulty translating the lines above his eyebrows when he told his team to go warm up.

Madeline wanted Coach Jones to understand her impression of Jarvis was a pleasant one: "Coach Jones, Jarvis is not the person you described."

Coach locked his jaws and glared at his girls, "Go warm up!"

Driven by winning, Coach Jones's philosophy was to motivate his athletes by viewing their competitors as the adversary. Madeline believed Jones made a lot of enemies because he "pulled his girls aside." He didn't want them socializing or interacting with anyone. Jarvis disagreed with Coach Jones's stance.

She formed a bond with Martha Watson, a long jumper from Long Beach Poly High School. Although they competed in different events, the two often spent quality time together at track meets. Whether it was under a shade tree or in the bleachers, they made sure it was within eyeshot of Coach Jones.

"We'd find a spot so we could keep our eyes on Fred. He was

like the Mother Duck. They would walk behind him in a line," Martha said.

While she did not agree with Fred, it was easy to pick up on his strategy. "He thought it would make them run faster against competitors," she said.

For Jarvis, she viewed her competitors differently.

"My toughest competitors were always my close friends," Jarvis said. "I've always understood that friends help friends push through the finish."

Whether you were black or white, Jarvis relished relationships. The racism and other inequities that loomed over the country did not matter. Not even when it came to white middle-distance runner Doris Brown (no relation to Reynaldo Brown). Jarvis believed that the racial climate could be an opportunity to embrace what most refused to acknowledge: Race and relationships.

"We are more alike than different, but it's time to face race. We can't keep saying that we don't see race, when it is evident that racism is real," Jarvis said.

Though some may have been apprehensive to talk about it, Jarvis found ways to demonstrate it. Recalling a speech from Dr. Martin Luther King Jr., she often said, "We must walk and live out our days together as brothers."

Jarvis modeled that truth with Doris Brown, and vice versa.

With her own childhood trials and trauma, Doris understood

what it meant to overcome: "It takes a challenge to bring the best out of someone."

Nothing stopped the white athletes from supporting their black teammates.

"If they couldn't go into a restaurant, we weren't going in either," Doris said.

The challenges they faced in the segregated south created a powerful connection. "People like Jarvis and Barb stood out," Doris said.

As much as Jarvis and Barb drew Doris's attention, the coaching style of Fred T. Jones was a walking billboard.

Although Doris admired Jones's ability to coach, she cringed at his ability to cultivate healthy relationships.

"I'm so glad Jarvis didn't allow Fred Jones's controlling personality to dictate the way she treated others. She was always encouraging to others and didn't get that from Fred," Doris declared.

"I always felt sorry for Jarvis and Barb because of the way he treated them. They trained hard and were outstanding people. We were happy to have the coaches we had. He terrified me."

"It's not that the other coaches weren't protective, but they allowed them to have a life," Madeline said. "Jones was a club coach and hovered over them. He didn't give them a chance to do the right thing because he assumed they would screw up. When he got mad at them, he snarled and gritted his teeth. He would get on them in front of people. ... He was hurtful."

And like her friend Jaye, Madeline always showed Coach Jones respect. "People didn't speak to him. I'm one of the few whom he didn't cut off," Madeline said.

"I met Jarvis by tearing the sheets off Jones. She liked me because I was honest and truthful. I liked her for the same reason. It was an honor to have a competitor bring out your best."

Not even the quest for a spot on the Olympic team in the same event could come between the two, because the foundation of their friendship was truth and trust. On or off the track, the two were committed to being there for one another. They were both willing to give and receive. And even if it were hard to hear, they would tell one another the truth.

Listening to the stories shared by Coach Scott and her friends reminded me of the messages that echoed in her coaching. Surround yourself with positive people. Don't allow others to distract you from your goals.

"If it means having one friend, learn to let go. And when you find that person who pours positivity in your life, plant your seed," Jarvis said.

From the moment Madeline and Jarvis met, it was clear they shared more than the 800 meters. They built an unbreakable bond that transcended the track.

So did Jarvis and Doris. "She was a special person, and made it despite, rather than because of," Doris said.

Regarding the challenges they faced, she said, "Sports brought us together, but it was the grace of God that kept us."

Good soil is the foundation of planting friendships. It lays the groundwork for relationships to flourish. And when bonds are strengthened, you will find friends that not only celebrate the wonderful moments in your life but they are with you in the wilderness. Everyone longs to have at least one loyal friend.

Another lesson that reverberated in Coach Scott's stories about her friends was not to minimize the race of others.

"I learned that being color-blind would never help to solve racism or unite our country," she said.

No longer would she allow others to deny the daily challenges of people of color that for so long had been minimized by four words: "I don't see color."

Instead, she would work hard to reinforce the importance of cross-cultural relationships. "When you have a genuine friendship with someone of another race, it's easier not to perpetuate stereotypes, prejudice, and racism. All of my friends made me a better person," Jarvis said.

Just as she enriched the lives of those around her.

Since none of us will journey through life alone, we can never underestimate the power of genuine friendships. They will empower and encourage you. Affirm and appreciate you. Genuine friends are honest, even when the truth hurts. They will not be envious of your

Friendship beyond the borders; Madeline Manning and Jarvis Scott (Mexico City, 1968)

Madeline at the Aztec Pyramids in Teotihuacan, Mexico (October, 1968)

Martha Watson 1968 Olympic team photo; Long Jump

Bonding to enhance team performance Mexico City (1968); From left Jarvis Scott, Barbara Ferrell, Iris Davis, Mamie Rallins, Doris Brown; Kneeling: Eleanor Montgomery elevation. With strong relationships you learn that when all hell is breaking loose, those people will stick by you and fight for and with you.

While you may not talk for days, months, or even years, genuine friendships never end. They create memories that will last forever.

Leadership Principle #4

The same can be said of strong leaders. Great leaders take the time to connect with people on a level that goes beyond the job description. They create a sense of community, mutual trust, and authenticity, without sacrificing their role as a leader.

Take a look at those on your team. What are you doing to build healthy relationships?

CHAPTER 5

The Call to Forgive

"After graduating from high school, car accidents, family problems, working, and a list of trials interrupted my progression in track. I had to learn how to move forward."—J

The Silent Scream

Before she turned the corner, a cold object rested at her throat. All the street smarts had not prepared her for the battle. Even still, the young black girl from Watts desperately wanted to scrap. When she could no longer feel the knife, she struggled to lose herself from his grip. She fought like hell!

For a split second, she freed herself. As the muscular man rushed toward her, sadly, her speed and strength were no match. He snatched her wrist and yanked her close. His bulging deep blue eyes were dark and evil. As she bit down on his hand, his cologne soaked her tongue.

"Bitch!" he yelled out.

Still, she continued to fight. While her gut-wrenching scream pierced his ears, a roar of thunder blocked her cry.

Her surroundings sped in circles. Short of breath, she gasped and then asked, "What do you want? I don't have any money."

His hardened manhood now pressed upon her. "I don't want your money. I want you, darkie," he whispered. His nostrils flared and breathing became labored, as once again, he yanked at her arms.

Tears flooded her face, yet she fixed her eyes heavenward.

"I decided if I looked to my God for help, He would save me. If He didn't save me, I prayed for strength to overcome it," Jarvis said.

The "blue-eyed demon" stripped the eighteen-year-old of her virginity. He pried her right leg open with his knee and held her arms in a locked position. As he penetrated her, she cried out. Still, no one heard her. She clenched her fist as tight as possible. No matter how hard she bit her bottom lip, the pain never eased. Each time he penetrated was like an excruciating stab.

When he finished, he warned her not to move.

She wasn't certain how much time had passed. Her surroundings no longer spinning, everything came into focus. Jarvis crawled over to the wall and clawed her hands up the cold brick and made her way upright. Tears still streaming down her eyes, she began fixing her clothes.

For a moment, everything froze. As she prepared to head home, shame weighed down upon her shoulders like the gnawing and ripping between her legs. The warmth running on the inside of her inner thigh was unsettling. She was not on her menstrual cycle. The skin hanging on the back of her hands was now secondary. As she looked down, an ominous red stain seeped through her skirt. After taking a few steps, she doubled over and vomited before falling to her knees.

Fearful of mistreatment and misperceptions, Jarvis decided not to go to the police. "Black woman and a white man. I cringed thinking how the story would play out."

The challenging and barrage of questions stood at the forefront of her mind.

"I had been victimized once and didn't want to go through it again. I could already see it coming. 'What were you wearing? Were you dating him? Where do you live? What were you doing on that side of town? Did you say no? How do you know he was white?'"

Justice, in her mind, would not prevail.

She made the conscious decision not to speak of the horrific trauma to anyone. But the grim reality of her silence couldn't do away with the image of the perpetrator's face; it would forever be engraved in her mind.

Jarvis would never forget his words. And feeling dirty and disgusted, she found little solace in the shower.

"More than anything, I wanted to get rid of his smell," she said.

"I scrubbed and scrubbed like I had never done before. I stopped scrubbing when my skin started burning from the lather."

For forty-eight days in a row, Jarvis replayed that sickening ordeal over and over in her mind. She no longer disregarded the tightening in her chest when she thought a white man was too close. The constant urge to fight was overwhelming, but she remembered something her grandmother often said: "To set yourself free, you got to forgive."

Determined that the ordeal would no longer eat away at the core of her soul, she realized she had to forgive the perpetrator and forgive herself. And she had to forgive herself for not telling anyone. Forgive herself for hating her body. Forgive herself for not fending off the perpetrator. Forgive herself for hating white men. The traumatic ordeal would no longer have power over her.

"I had to find peace in my dark valley ... I had to let it go," she insisted.

Tucked away in her purse, she would keep the words of the Apostle Paul on a piece of paper: "Therefore, there is now no condemnation for those who are in Christ Jesus." (Romans 8:1)

Forgiveness seemed like a journey. The unpacking of the emotional baggage seemed to weigh less and less. The process was painful, but it was a gift that Jarvis believed she had to give herself.

I remember her words so vividly: "I was helpless, and a white man was having me without my consent."

My heart grieved for Coach Scott. But amid my tears I learned that I grieved for myself too. I learned that my grief looked different because I had surrendered to hurt and pain. I had not given myself the gift of forgiveness in some areas of my life. I could no longer rehearse the hurt. It was time to release.

Unforgiveness is like a misfired nerve ending. The physical pain may start in one area of our lives, but it can trigger in other areas ... social, emotional, financial, etc.

Coach Scott's prayer for strength to move beyond the sexual assault exemplifies what I believe is a declaration to dwell in safety. The wonderful news is we have assurance that "When you pass through the rivers, they will not overwhelm you; when you walk through the fire, you shall not be burned, and the flame shall not consume you." (Isaiah 43:2)

First, we should recognize that troubles are inevitable. The prophet Isaiah begins the scripture with "When," showing expectation. It may not be sexual assault, but there is an appointed day and time for troubles to come your way.

Second, Isaiah reminds us the very thing intended to destroy will not devour us. Oh, to walk through fire and come out not smelling like smoke! When we are kept by Jesus, he clothes us with flame-retardant materials that no manufacturer can duplicate!

Jarvis used her setbacks as a guide. Years later she would help others to heal by becoming a surrogate mother, counselor, and friend to young female and male athletes who had personal struggles. Coach Scott demonstrated vulnerability as she shared her story with survivors of sexual assault and other forms of abuse. And for those whose trauma was unrelated to sexual assault, she found a way to aid and restore their hurting hearts by listening, empathizing, and demonstrating unconditional love.

How did she heal from her hurt? Lifting her small King James Bible, she said, "I used my pain for His glory."

Leadership Principle #5

You can do the same. Great leaders use their pain for a purpose bigger than themselves. Great leaders forgive. No matter the hurt, they don't harbor anger.

It's difficult for leaders to forgive others if they can't forgive themselves. Guilt prevents you from not only being the best you but giving that to others. Forgiveness opens the way to healing and growth. Great leaders also help to facilitate the act of forgiveness. They acknowledge pain and hurt and use it as a springboard to move forward and create a judgment-free zone and an environment for reconciliation.

CHAPTER 6

The Call to Set Goals

> *"I will never give up on a goal that I have set for myself.*
> *I will stand back and check the balance of my goals to*
> *see (1) where I started to where I am now in reaching*
> *my accomplishment and (2) how much more work I*
> *have to complete before I reach my goals."—J*

Set up for Success

Doris and Jarvis lined up against one another at the AAU (Amateur Athletic Union) Championships in Santa Barbara. The two vied for a spot to the 1967 Pan Am Games in Winnipeg, Canada. Doris was in lane one. Neck in neck, Jarvis and Doris battled for the finish line. The photographer wanted the perfect shot and stood in lane one to capture the finish. Doris pumped her arms as she ran the final 100 meters toward the finish line. She had a choice to run over him or run around him, but a misstep rendered disqualification.

Doris placed second in the event but felt bad for beating her friend and competitor. She will always remember Jarvis being a wonderful sport.

"I had better times, but she respected the loss. If I wanted to make the team, I had to beat her," she said. Doris paused. "I can't say enough about Jarvis. She made everyone feel special. Distance runner Lynn Jennings used to say, 'Honor your competitors with your best effort.' Jarvis did just that. We didn't climb over teammates to get where we were going. We didn't do that in track."

Jarvis knew that doing her best also meant accepting the loss as a normal part of competition. She didn't allow the setback of not qualifying for the Pan Am Games to shake her confidence.

"The spirit of a warrior cannot break," she said. "In the face of disappointment I may be shaken, but never broken. Dreams fall short, but we revamp, make changes, and go forth."

Instead of focusing on the loss at the AAU Championships in 1967, Jarvis began to practice goal setting and journaling in August 1967. She wrote about each workout, the times as well as the results from track meets, on a yellow legal pad. She also penned her thoughts and personal affirmations on a separate pad.

For instance, on her legal pad she wrote about a workout from October 21, 1967. She ran four sets of eight 220s. Thirty-two times running half the distance of the track took her a while. On October 24, she ran eighteen 330s. The distance began at the starting line and ended at the last curve before the home stretch.

Though some of the workouts took quite some time to complete, Jarvis's buddy Barb waited for her to finish.

After the October 24th workout, she wrote on her legal pad, "The most serious challenge often overlooked is becoming skilled and trained in goal setting and to get the most out of myself. Keep pushing."

Years later, the practice of goal setting and affirmations continued. Following her workout on November 6, 1975, she wrote, "See yourself on a program of hard work. ... How you live and what you do during that time determines the greatness you achieve. It must convince you shortcuts to success are nonexistent."

Coach Scott stayed focused on her personal goals. Big or small she didn't allow setbacks or losses to hinder her progress. She learned those lessons from her father's staunch belief about bed making.

Ivory Scott taught his children that bigger goals were attainable when smaller tasks became important. A disciplinarian in every sense of the word, he ran the household like a platoon. No basic training was necessary, because Ivory would incorporate his practices in the home any and every way possible.

Consequently, the fitted sheet was tucked firmly under the

Doris Brown,
1968 Olympic
Team photo

Pan Am Games
Winnipeg, 1967;
Madeline Manning,
1st Place and Doris
Brown, 2nd Place

Write the vision

10-10-67

A handwritten running/training log organized in a grid of dated cells.

Sept. 19 – Tues	Sept 21 Thurs	Sept. 22 Fri	Sept. 26 Tues	Sept 27 wed	Sept 30 Sat	Oct 3	Oct 4
6 laps cross country Course	Cross County Course	2 set of Kent 330's Track	Cross Country Course	10 (2 30's) Time Trials Track	4 (220's) not going in + 30 yd out all out 110 on hard surf	9 long laps	Time Trials one 440
10-10-67 Tues Cross County	10-11-67 windsprints Time 220	Cross County	10-14-67 3 (60's) with time 220 220 in between Time 440	10-21-67 4 set of 8 all out 300 35 in all	10-24-67 (8 330's) running in place with 11 laps	10-25-67 (12 (100's) time 880	10-28-67 6 hills ran them good
10-31-67 2 set of 330's 6 in a set	11-1-67 5 hills (6 (660's) Cool out 4 hills	11-2-67 4 hills	11-7-67 14 (220's) 3 set of 8 Set ups	11-14-67 1 set of 330's Time Trials 660-440-220-100	11-14-67 20 (160's) 2 set cont 330's 6 in a set 12 (100's)	11-15-67	11-18-67 40 (60) running place
11-21-67 4 hills	11-22-67 windsprints 10 laps Running in place	11-24-67 No time Trials Cont 660 (440) 330	11-25-67 33 (220)	11-28-67 25 (160's with trot)	12-5-67 30 (220's)	12-5-67 10 (440) 12 (50's)	12-6-67 4 (660's) 2 miles
12-9-67 3 (660's) 1 (440) 8 (50's) 12 (110's)	12-12-67 15 (330's)	25 (220's) Good flight 1½ laps cool out	Track Meet 10 (100's) 440–560 220–255 Hawthorne	12-14-67 5 (330's) Trot 5 (220's) eat 6 (110's) 6 (160's)	12-12-6 7 (440's) 8 (330's)	12-27-6 1 (660) 10 (110's) 10 (110's)	
12-26-67 40 (50's)	12-27-67 11 (440's) 6 laps	12-28-67 43 (220's) 6 laps	12-29-67 1 set of cont 330's 12 (300's)	12-30-67 1 (660) 1 (440) 24 laps	12-14-67 Run for 30 Min. running in place 8 (50's) 3 laps	1-3-68 1 set cont 330's 11 330's 200 Jumping	
1-4-68 1660 trot 200–1 (660 trot 220 all out 220) 110 trot	all 440 15 (110's) 1 330	1-5-68 3 (660's) 30 (110's) all out 1	1-6-67 1 (880) inst of 1 (660) windsprints 1 (440) 1 (330) 1 (220) 1 (110)	1-9-68 2 set of Kent's 330's 10 in a set 1 lap	1-10-68 8 (110's) 110–run 30 out 110–run 30 out 110–run 30 out 110–run sweeter	Run fast 15 yrs 15 (50's) set 5 laps	
1-13-68 Ran in Circular 300 & 375 880 (3rd)	1-15-68 2 set of Kent 360 1 set of 10 2 set of...	1-11-68 2 set of Kent 330 set of 10 run 440 trot 110 run 330 trot 110 run 330 trot 110 run 330 trot 110	run 440 out 110 run 330 trot 110 run 330 trot 110	10 (160's) 3 laps	1-17-68 40 (110's)	1-22-68 Exercises	1-23-68 2 sets of 330's 440 6 in the curve 6 laps
7-25-68 2 set of 330's (cont) 1 set of 10 1 set of 6 6 laps	1-24-68 Albuquerque 2.17.6 880	1-29-68 24 (220's) 12 in a set	1-30-68 4 (660's) 10 laps windsprints 12 laps Cool out	1-31-68 12 (440's) 6 laps	2-1-68 40 (110's)	2-3-68 Track meet San Diego 880 (2.13.3)	2-5-68 2 set of cont 330's 6 (50's) 6 laps
2-6-68 12 440's trot 110 5 (100's) 10 jungle jungles	2-7-68 1 (660) 1 (660's) 1 (440) 1 (330) 5 (cool out 110's)	2-8-68 15 (110's)	set run 2-10-68 880 2. M.4 Forum	2-12-68 4 (440) 7 (330's cont)	2-13-68 30 (220's)	2-14-68 40 (220's)	2-15-68 3 (500's) 15 (110's on curve

mattress, and it had to be smooth. The next sheet had to have square corners, and the folds had to be at 45-degree angles. Uniformity was a must; the sheets nor the blankets could have wrinkles. Not even the slightest bit of gathering was allowed. Nothing was out of place—the pillows would also be centered neatly next to one another.

Once the beds were made, there would be no napping during the day. In the morning, as soon as the Scott children's feet touched the floor, bed making would commence. Why? Because Ivory believed it would set the tone for the rest of the day. He didn't want his children to be idle. While the bed making was initially a hard task, the Scott children set small goals around bed making until it became routine. Ivory was simply teaching his children the importance of paying attention to detail. He also wanted them to understand the importance of perseverance.

Jarvis always believed that he wanted every one of them to know that even the small and mundane things had significance. More importantly, he wanted them to understand that if you can't complete small tasks, you will never be able to set and endure to be able to achieve the big things.

Jarvis attributed her commitment to write her vision to her father. "Who would've thought bed making could teach us about setting goals? His insight was impeccable!" she said with a beaming smile.

Setting goals and workouts and perseverance paid huge dividends. Jarvis placed first in the 400 meters at the Women's

Nationals in Denver in 1968. The Women's Olympic Team Trials in Walnut, California, convened at Mt. San Antonio College (Mt. SAC). She qualified for the Olympic Team, taking 1st in the 400 meters and 3rd in the 800 meters.

When I was on her team, even though we weren't training for the Olympics, performance was no doubt important to Coach Scott. But learning was even more paramount with mastery of goals.

"Some people spend more time and energy trying to gain strength and improve their performance than seeking mastery of goals," she said.

In hindsight, I see how she was trying to prepare us for something beyond sport, and beyond her time here on earth. She was so committed to goal setting that she wanted us at some point in our lives to reflect on goals from years past.

In her home office, she kept files of practically all her student-athletes. Flipping through the folders I began to think how, regardless of our win-loss record, goal setting was a regimen. Kicking off the year, she would write outlooks for each of us that included goals sheets to write the times and/or marks we were hoping to achieve. The sheet also included a comment section for the athlete and coach. She returned the goals sheets after each meet with a response related to our progress. Or a lack thereof. At the top of each goal sheet read, "Before you win, you must learn to lose."

Coach Scott did not want her girls to possess a "woe is me"

mentality. After a loss, assessing our goals would include reflecting on the previous race or field event. Learning to lose meant taking accountability for what happened in our race or field event. She was trying to teach us to deal with the emotions but keep our focus on the mark.

One of my teammates, Georgianna Jones, was a quarter-miler and middle-distance runner from Queen City, Texas, near the borders with Arkansas and Louisiana. On January 24, 1987, Texas Tech hosted an Invitational Indoor Track Meet. Georgianna made it to the finals and Coach Scott assessed her race.

"I'm proud of you," Coach wrote. "We are nearing a point of gaining strength and competitive intensity. We have additional levels and heights to meet."

There were even times when Coach Scott felt the need to write on our goal sheets after watching us practice. For example, on February 12, 1987, she wrote to Georgianna, "There was no fire in you today. Work on your concentration. Don't over-express warming up all day but learn to use quality warm-ups and build yourself up so you can be ready to go. Give yourself quiet time to get ready. We need to develop a serious side of our approach."

And in losses, she took the time to let us know that she appreciated our efforts. At the end of the 1987 indoor track season, she wrote to Georgianna, "Well, kid, you have been a joy to work with and watch grow. I, and a few others, believe that your talent has been untapped, and when you learn to compete on a quality level, you will have a grand future. Thanks for your patience and cooperation. Coach Scott."

The first time I saw my file and copies of goal sheets was twenty-five years after graduating.

While visiting Coach Scott at her home, she said, "Come back here, Tiger. Let me show you something."

She walked into her office, opened the file cabinet, and handed me the manila file. My eyes beamed. I sat on the floor and began reading some of the goal sheets.

The first paper was a goal sheet for the San Angelo Relays. I was scheduled to compete in the 400 meters, mile relay, long jump, and triple jump. I giggled as I looked at my goal. I had written on my goal sheet, "I will not show any pain." Coach Scott's response was, "Please be specific." It began to feel as though it was yesterday that she called me over and began to explain her response: "If you're not clear, you won't know how to get there."

After the Texas Tech Invitational on January 24, 1987, Coach Scott wrote, "You have a tiger in your tank when you are running. Keep your eye on your grades and work harder. Athletically, you are sound." She saw my potential before I saw it in myself.

On February 12, 1987, she provided encouragement by writing, "It has been a delight to see you progress to this point. Your toughness as an athlete will be your key of improvement as we compete with stronger and faster athletes. Your future here at Texas Tech is looking very bright."

Even during hard periods such as injury, gratitude filled her heart. "I am very glad that your injury was not serious. I wouldn't know how to handle it if it was to take you out for a length of time. You just got too much going for you to have to go through a terrible season. Thanks for being a trooper."

We learned to respond to setbacks, whether it was in the form of losing a race, an injury, academic probation, loss of a job, unemployment, divorce, or other trials. Who better to learn from than the woman whose training ground began in Waco and continued in Watts and Lubbock? Every racial encounter, experience with prejudice, and obstacle taught her preemptive strikes were fruitless if goal setting didn't follow.

Georgianna and I; Determined to reach our goals at the 1987 Southwest Conference Championships in Austin, TX

Georgianna Jones at practice

Excited about the journey toward new goals: Southwest Conference Indoor Meet in Fort Worth, TX.

Leadership Principle #6

To give team members a sense of direction, effective leaders push their team to set goals and objectives. Even if team members have a setback, goal setting will trigger behavior that motivates them to push. Because they have a sense of direction, team members are more likely to put forth effort.

Strong leaders also make sure that the goals and objectives are specific. General goals such as "I will do my best" do not aid with increasing motivation and don't provide direction on how to obtain the goal. If you can't measure the goal, neither team members nor the leader will know if the team member is doing well.

When leaders give timely and accurate feedback to goals that their team members set, it helps the team member to adapt and make the necessary changes to help reach their target. Feedback helps the team to identify strengths and areas of improvement and lets the team member know that you care and are invested in their personal and professional growth.

Why not begin today?

CHAPTER 7

The Call to Become Part of the Solution

> *"I hope to be an agent of change in our families and communities."*—J *(March 27, 2010)*

A Year to Remember

Before the Scott family could sit at the dinner table on April 4, 1968, and two days before Jarvis's twenty-first birthday, sorrow ripped through the home. Shards of glass and ice cubes from the jelly jar covered the floor. The red Kool-Aid stained Johnnie Mae Scott's apron.

"My dad embraced Mama as she wept," said Jarvis, sobbing.

On the balcony of the Lorraine Motel, the dream vanished. The murder of Dr. Martin Luther King Jr. in Memphis not only devastated the Scott family but changed the trajectory of the civil rights movement in the United States.

And then, like a repetitive blow to an open wound, the news of Robert F. Kennedy's assassination inflamed scars in the black community. Losing the presidential candidate dimmed the hope for healing and reconciliation. While no declaration of a public health scare filled the airwaves, the wounds from discrimination, racism, police brutality, and many other injustices had become infectious.

Still, many hoped for a panacea. A beacon of light illuminated hope from the darkness that loomed in the United States. The XIX Olympiad in Mexico City began on October 12, 1968. Bent, but not broken, dismayed, but not deterred, black athletes became more vocal. Shut up and run would not be their montage. They began to express concern and outrage about the exploitation of black athletes.

On many college campuses across the country, black student-athletes were celebrated for their athletic abilities, but their experiences outside the sports arena were a stark contrast. They were treated like second-class citizens, subjected to racial slurs, denied housing, and banned from entering some restaurants.

Now, when witnessing the plight of the black male athlete, Jarvis and her female counterparts kept their frustration in check.

"They treated our men like kings overseas, but inhumanely in our country," Madeline Manning-Mims said.

Madeline recalled the discrepancy in treatment for black male athletes compared to white male athletes. Take, for example, high schooler and white distance runner Jim Ryan.

In a matter-of-fact tone, she said, "Still in high school, he had an entourage. He was on the way to be the best, but we were already the best!"

Although seventeen years old, high jump phenom Reynaldo Brown also recognized the disparate treatment. He stayed under the wings of San Jose sprinter John Carlos, who was also a member of the Olympic Project for Human Rights (OPHR). A junior in high school, Reynaldo listened and observed.

"I never said a word, but now see history is repeating itself," he said.

Athletes, black and white, gathered to discuss the possibility of boycotting the 1968 Olympic Games. The Olympic Project for Human Rights was founded by Harry Edwards. A 1964 graduate of San Jose State and a 1968 Olympic participant, Edwards was concerned about the disparate treatment of blacks. The organization wanted five demands to be met. They wanted more black coaches to be hired, and they wanted Muhammad Ali's heavyweight boxing title to be restored. Ali's title was stripped because he had refused to enter the military draft to fight in the Vietnam War.[10]

The black athletes also called for the firing of Avery Brundage, the head of the United States Olympic Committee, because of his white supremacist stance. In addition, they wanted Rhodesia and South Africa's invitation to compete in the Olympics to be withdrawn because of their participation in apartheid. Last, they called for a boycott of the New York Athletic Club, because of the organization's discriminatory and racist policies. The club's membership policy prohibited black, Puerto Rican, and Jewish athletes but didn't mind profiting from them competing in their annual indoor track meet.[11]

But 1936 Olympian and four-time gold medalist Jesse Owens, who experienced the racism of Hitler firsthand, spoke to the US team and urged them not to boycott. Instead, he encouraged them to use their athletic talents as their voice. While some felt as though Owens was being used by Brundage, they decided to compete.

During the second team meeting, athletes agreed that individuals should "do their own thing." They also agreed to wear black clothing items of their choice as a silent protest.

The women didn't play much of a role in the discussions. "There wasn't a lot determined from us," Madeline said. "Only one time the team came together, men and women, black and white. They told us it was up to us as individuals, and we wouldn't face consequences for our actions. Because of that, it drew the team close together."

Jarvis saw it differently: "They didn't bother to ask the women about it." She believed the contributions of women were diminished.

The host city of the 1968 Olympics had its share of problems. Gunfire rang out while thousands of students protested the Mexican government. Countless students shot and killed ... unarmed ... unnamed ... and the perpetrators unpunished. Tremors from the devastation in Mexico reached the United States.[12]

"We heard about what happened to the Mexican students, but the press tried to keep it hush, hush," Reynaldo said.

The racial tension in the United States, coupled with the oppression of Mexicans in Mexico City, left a hole in the hearts and minds of many. And yet, hope soared that the 19th Olympic Games would teach valuable lessons beyond the Olympic Village or Olympic sport venues, promoting peace and a sense of sisterhood and brotherhood that would echo throughout the world.

How? I'm glad you asked. Although the women were not included in all of the discussions, that did not stop Jarvis from responding. She made the decision to participate in the Olympic Games.

Her decision-making process was simple: "Compete or go home."

She carefully weighed the alternatives. Going home would not help shine the light on the inequities and inequalities.

"I decided to use my platform," she said.

If Coach Scott were here today, she would say "find a way." She always encouraged us to look for ways to play an active role in addressing problems. Perhaps that's why when there was conflict on the team, she'd wait for us to work it out. Even if it meant stewing in silence for hours while traveling to a track meet, so be it. She would encourage us to use the tools she gave us and find a way to create positive change.

With increased racial tension and chaos around her following King's assassination, Jarvis saw the need to create change. Amidst the political and racial climate, she still saw an opportunity. She seized every opportunity to better those around her. Not only was she at the right place, at the right time but present for "a time such as this."

Jarvis Scott, 1968 Olympic team photo

Ready to represent at the Opening Ceremonies (Mexico City, 1968); From left: Jarvis Scott, Barbara Ferrell, and Madeline Manning

Leadership Principle #7

A key leadership principle is understanding that leading is not about us. Instead, it is about serving. True leadership means being courageous and willing to face problems head-on. True leadership means having a willingness to sacrifice. It means addressing problems by becoming part of the solution.

Are you part of the problem or are you part of the solution?

"It was difficult during that period," Jarvis said.

No matter what, she remained committed to her country even though the country she represented was unfaithful to her and other black athletes.

Was she willing to act? The honor was all hers. The opportunity awaits you too!

CHAPTER 8

The Call to Selfless Humility

> *"I don't know of any virtuous characteristic*
> *than to put others before yourself."—J*

Serve

After opening the plastic storage box, my attention immediately fixated on the cardboard that lay across the bin full of mementos. Handwritten with black marker, it read, "Jarvis Scott. High School, USA Teams, 400-meter final–1968. Qualified in two events, 400 meters/800 meters 1968. Save forever."

Becoming the first American female athlete to do so, Jarvis qualified for the 1968 Olympic Games in the 400 meters and 800 meters. The Olympic Trials for the women were held at Mt. SAC in California. Jarvis placed first in the 400 meters and third in the 800 meters.

Fiddling through the papers and magazines, I pulled out a blue sheet dated October 15, 1968. It was the heat sheet for the semifinals of the 400 meters at the 1968 Olympics. At the top it read, "JUEGOS DE LA XIX OLIMPIADA–MEXICO." Faded typed letters, but still legible, the notes that Coach Jones wrote on the semifinals heat sheet hypnotized me. On the front of the heat sheet was a hand drawn diagram of an oval track. On the blue-colored sheet, Coach Jones wrote reminder notes to Jarvis.

At 300 meters, an arrow marked the spot to remind Jarvis, "Now I'm going to feel good. Gather."

On the back side of the heat sheet, Coach Jones wrote more notes to Jarvis and Barb: "I have prayed for both of you. Jarvis Barb Eat Big. A must for total strength." Another note said, "Barb runs semis and the run for the gold off of lunch. You must be determined and enthusiastic. You must be happy about it."

Indeed, Barbara Ferrell reaped the benefits of her labor, earning a silver medal in the 100 meters and a gold medal in the 4x100 meter relay.

The heat sheet for the 400-meter finals had similar notes. "Action in knees and pound for extension," Coach Jones wrote. "Working up strength. They'll be inching up. Must keep lift. Must keep mechanics. Foot pound extension. All piston. No extension."

He directed the last word of encouragement to Jarvis and

Barbara: "Be like coach-Nasty and hard to get along with. The coaches STARE. Evil eye."

The gun sounded, and the runners exploded out of the starting blocks. The finals of the 400-meter race took place on October 16, 1968. Wearing bib number 102, Jarvis was in lane four. The "black" shorts went unnoticed. She was the first American female athlete to make the finals in the 400 meters.

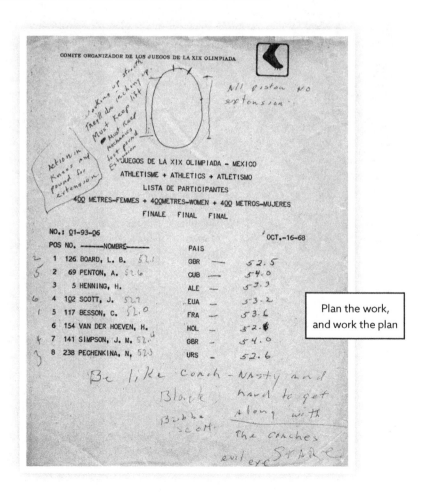

"Jarvis Scott is in the lead!" the announcer said. The first 200 meters was blazing. "USA! USA!" the crowd roared.

In the final 50 meters, her arms continued to pump, but runners began to pass her on the right. Crossing the finish line with a personal best of 52.8, it wasn't the race that she and Coach Jones had strategized.

1968 Olympics, Mexico City, 400 meter finals

"I didn't run my race," said Jarvis, who placed sixth.

The second race was the 800 meters. No American female had ever run both events in the Olympics. Jarvis should have been entered. According to USA Track and Field, Madeline Manning placed first at the 1968 Olympic Track and Field Trials; Doris Brown placed second, Jarvis Scott third, and Francie Kraker placed fourth.[13]

But humility settled in her soul. In an act of solidarity, Jarvis had gifted teammate Francie Kraker an opportunity to compete on the Olympic team. The University of Michigan half-miler would not have to wait another four years to try-out for the Olympic team. But thanks to Jarvis, the dream would not be deferred.

Barbara Ferrell grappled with her friend and teammate about relinquishing such an honor.

"She had trained very hard for the double," Barbara said. "They spoke to Jaye and asked her to give up the spot. Next, Francie approached Jaye and asked her to give it up. Jaye was such a giving person. They tried to say the races were too close in being run, not giving Jarvis enough time to recuperate."

Barbara sighed.

"All that work Jaye did to give it up to that girl. I thought she could do it," said Barbara, who stood in awe of Jarvis's work ethic. "We'd get to the practice and Jaye was already running. We'd leave, and she'd still be running."

Coach Jones struggled with Jarvis giving up her spot. "I was so hurt," he said when we spoke on October 15, 2017, forty-nine years to the day of the 400-meter semifinals. "Jarvis was the most athletic and hardworking athlete I'd ever coached."

Forty-nine years later, Coach Jones was adamant that Jarvis was asked to go on runs with a few other distance runners so they could convince her to give up her spot in the 800 to Francie.

"She had never gone against me. She was just a giving person," he said. "There was no changing her mind. She put in hard work every day and gave it up to that white girl."

Madeline believed in Jarvis's strength and endurance. "Everybody had their opinions. I had mine but didn't voice it. I didn't have her position," Madeline said. "Everyone on the staff was getting impatient with her putting it off. The next thing, Jarvis decided to concentrate on the 400, so Francie could pull up to the third spot for the American entrants in the event."

"That was something to do," Reynaldo Brown said, regarding Jarvis's selfless act. "She had worked so hard, but she was just that person to give to someone else."

Martha Watson did not know when Jarvis made the decision. "I just know when Francie made the team, Jarvis had given up her spot. No one deserved to be there more than Jarvis," Martha said.

Much like Madeline, Doris Brown didn't give her opinion: "It wasn't my business, and I just stayed out of it." She paused. "Francie knew how to go after what she wanted. She laid it on thick."

But Doris understood the act: "It was a really, really great and amazing thing that Jarvis did it. It was even more amazing that Fred let her do it. He didn't have a say, but you just didn't go against him. To stand up to Fred was amazing! It was honorable."

Madeline Manning went on to win the gold medal in the 800 meters, setting an Olympic record of 2:00.9. Doris Brown placed fifth in the same event with a time of 2:03.9.

Martha Watson placed tenth in the long jump with a mark of 6.20 meters. And as the youngest male US Olympian, seventeen-year-old Reynaldo Brown placed ninth. If only the internalization had not affected his performance.

"I didn't want to win because I didn't believe it would mean anything," he said. "I wanted what the whites got. But the job offers, money, and commercials wouldn't be available to blacks."

Jarvis never wavered about her rationale for giving up her spot in the 800 meters. "I wanted to give another American an opportunity to achieve their goal and dream," she said.

Coach Jones still had the fire when we talked about that decision a second time.

"I believe that she could not just do it (by running in both events) but I thought she could win," he said. "That gold medal would have given her the title as one of the greatest ever in the sport. It shattered me. Jarvis had never gone against me."

When I first learned about Coach Scott giving up her Olympic spot, I was shocked, proud, and honored. Jarvis, nor the media, publicized her selfless act. Many friends, athletes, and teammates never knew. With the men's Olympic Trials being held in another state, it was easy for such an act of selflessness to go unnoticed. Instead of parading her actions, she minimized it and relished in watching another person achieve their dream.

She rarely mentioned it. Countless times Coach Scott and I talked about the gift of humility. It was as though she wanted one message, and one message only, to come out of her selfless act.

A warrior understands that he will be rewarded for noble deeds. How do I know? Because as she reminded me, "Great leaders ask the difficult questions of themselves."

Unsure of the question, I asked her to expound.

"What are you willing to give up for someone else to win?" she said.

Coach Scott understood that the heart of a strong leader begins with selflessness and humility. "One without the other won't do," she'd say.

Leadership Principle #8

Leadership is servanthood. The ultimate leader is one who is willing to be a servant to something bigger than themselves. They put the success of the team in front of their personal desires and out of the spotlight. Like Coach Scott, leaders serve because they not only want to grow people but they desire to give to people.

It is easy to recognize a good leader versus a great leader. Even when chaos is all around, great leaders respond with humility. And it is humility that ignites selflessness.

CHAPTER 9

The Call to Focus

"The joy I get out of coaching is watching athletes reach their full potential, earn a college degree, and then carry their experiences into life outside of the university."—J

First Encounter

Following the Olympics, Jarvis went on to represent the United States internationally. She also went back to complete her education at Cal State Los Angeles in 1975. An unconventional student-athlete, she was twenty-eight years old when she won the Association for Intercollegiate Athletics for Women (AIAW) Championships in Oregon. After graduating, she was offered an assistant coach position at her alma mater. Her presence at the 1979 AIAW Outdoor Track and Field Championships would foreshadow her later ascension as head coach at Texas Tech—the first African American head coach at the university. And it would forever be imprinted in the minds of her future track team members in the telling of the following story shared by Sharon Moultrie.

At those AIAW Championships, top athletes from across the country vied for a team and individual title at Michigan State University.

For freshman long jumper Sharon Moultrie, it was a fast break attack—to secure food and drink. She wrote up the play. Teammate Jennifer Perdue held possession of the keys, making a trip to 7-Eleven a seamless transition. Execute, execute, execute. With no time to scan the store, everyone agreed. In ... out ... back to the hotel. Break!

New city, new position; Jarvis Scott's 1st year at Texas Tech University (1979)

The van doors slammed as they ran into the store. Neither the scuffle in the parking lot nor the sound of screeching tires alarmed the girls.

Luckily, the slow traffic inside the store made for a quick exit.

"Two pops. Anything else for yuh?" the cashier said.

"Ten dollars on pump two," one customer said. Another customer headed to the checkout.

As the refrigerated door closed behind Sharon, she brimmed with pride as she shifted the six-pack in her arms and cruised toward the register. If only she had seen the customer in the aisle.

Mellow, yet confident. "Hey ladies! What are you all doing?" Her tall, erect posture and lackluster smile gave an air of authority. The beer and Boone's Farm exposed the play. "Are you competing in the track meet?"

Voices quivered. "Uh ... yes ma'am," they said.

"What school are you from and who is your coach?"

Before they responded, she scolded them. "You put those drinks back!"

As she headed to the door, she said, "Get focused ... and I will tell your coach!"

While sitting in the stands the next day, Jennifer kept going back and forth to the restroom. Sharon never watched the meet as her meaningless babble helped to distract Coach Beta, head women's track coach at Texas Tech University. Although they left East Lansing without being exposed, reprieve turned out to be temporary.

Fast-forward to September 1979, when Jarvis Scott began her duties as the head women's track and field coach at Texas Tech University. The track team wasn't the reigning Southwest Conference Champions, nor were they formidable enough to bid for such a title. Walking into the track stadium, Jarvis replayed her father's words in her head: "Leave your ego behind and let your actions speak for themselves."

Nestled behind the bleachers, the locker room blended in with the rest of the campus' Spanish Renaissance architecture. The men's track team entered from the south entrance and baseball from the north entrance. And from the east side of the building, the women entered the restroom that served as the locker room.

Jarvis jogged a mile around the track and headed back to her office.

Moments later, silence met Jarvis when she entered the J. T. King conference room. A West Texas chill swept through the room, postures stiffened, and eyes froze open.

Someone blurted, "That's the lady we saw at the convenient store!"

The color drained out of Jennifer's face.

Coach Scott's encouragement during the team meeting caused tension and uncertainty to fill the air.

"I need everybody to go buy Geritol!"

Muttering began. "W-What?" "Huh?" Some girls shook their heads in disbelief.

"Geritol?" they asked.

After the team meeting, the ladies hung out in the restroom and talked trash.

"She must be crazy!"

"How is she going to tell us we need to get Geritol?!"

The chatter, murmurs, and mimicking flooded the restroom. Commodes flushed and bathroom doors slammed open and shut. As some girls stood washing their hands, others pinned their hair. A few sat on the countertop.

Whoosh! Soon, the last commode flushed, and she exited the stall, stunning the girls. Jarvis stood 5 feet 8. A stopwatch and whistle dangled around her neck and shades clasped on her jacket.

"Yes, that's what I said!"

Time proved that the young athletes needed more than a supplement to make it through the daily workouts. And while some quit the team, the new head coach continued to caution against underestimating the value of vitamins.

"If you're deficient, you will feel it!"

Jennifer Perdue

Ready for take off; Sharon Moultrie competes in the long jump at an outdoor track meet

"Once I graduated from high school, I had academic and athletic scholarships. I experienced a lot of suffering, so I made a choice to drop out of school. I later continued my education and graduated from a junior college and a major university. My education had become more important than athletics. Once I accomplished my goals, I worked toward helping others with their goals and dreams."—J

Academics

At the start of each semester, we assembled in the J. T. King Room. The movie theatre seating was plush compared to the bleachers at the track. Excitement filled the room at seeing one another after the winter or summer break. The throwers sat with throwers, distance runners with distance runners, sprinters with sprinters, and so forth.

Coach Scott strutted in the room. There was a bounce and rhythm to her step. I loved her style. The confidence in her voice oozed. She encouraged us to excel in track and field, but academics was paramount.

"You are here to get an education. I'm not your mama and I'm not your daddy, but your parents entrusted you to me, and that makes you my responsibility," she said.

The candidness matched her compassion.

For example, during the spring semester, in 1987, the

administration at Texas Tech sent out a letter to the head coaches requesting a brief statement regarding their policy on study hall absences.

Coach Scott replied: "I don't know, but it will be severe. We have wasted money and time to offer opportunities for student-athletes to gain an education."

Coach Scott required all freshmen on the track team to attend study hall. By day, chatter and the smell of an array of foods filled Wiggins Dining Hall. During the evening, the aroma from dinner lingered, but they converted the dining facility to study hall for all sports. A semester GPA below 2.5 landed us back in study hall. No tutors on hand nor an elaborate system in place. Student-athletes just showed up and studied.

I never missed study hall, but my grades showed otherwise. I had become a shell while pledging a little sister organization. Perfect class attendance wasn't enough to keep me from academic probation. When I got the call and heard her voice on the other end, I knew it wasn't a courtesy call. There was no small talk.

"If you keep it up, you'll be home before you are officially accepted into the organization," Coach Scott said.

Although I wanted to become an active member, if I didn't make the adjustments, the opportunity to become a student-athlete would be lost.

Jarvis made sure that regardless of race or athletic abilities, we left Texas Tech with a degree. Did every one of us graduate? No, but she fought for each one of us, often reminding us that education was the key: "Once you get it, no one can take it away."

> *"Please keep us on your mailing list. Budget cost is a problem now, but for the future, we are hoping we can be able to schedule your meet."—J*

No Money, No Problem

Coach Scott also fought for a workable budget. The women's track program had little money. Just ask Sharon. She was in the first cohort of Coach Scott's student-athletes to experience the shortage.

"They didn't give her much money to recruit. She had to move around money to compete outside of West Texas," Sharon said.

Money woes meant that "other duties, as assigned" could include anything from helping Jarvis drive the vans to coaching any given event. Jan Chesbro, a graduate assistant for the women's team, could also relate.

"Unfortunately, the only time we flew the friendly skies was to the Cross Country and Indoor or Outdoor National Championships," said Jan, who helped coach all the field events except for the javelin.

Beale Tolbert agreed. She landed the assistant coach position in 1982.

"Try bringing in an athlete that had been to the University of Texas at Austin," she said.

That sprawling campus was no comparison to the landscape of the R. P. Fuller Track at Texas Tech.

"We had that ugly green fence that lined the entire track," Beale said.

The recruitment strategy required alterations. The twenty-five-year-old Beale did not have the athletic résumé as Jarvis, but she knew West Texas. Gifted at recruiting, she outworked others.

"We had to sell knowledge," she said. "We knew we had to out-smart everyone. (Jarvis) wanted the top ten, but most likely would not get them. We were bringing in kids on a bus, while others were bringing them in on planes. She either got the hard-working that were not elite or sometimes the elite that didn't want to work. That woman was tough!"

Jarvis's goals were realistic and attainable: "We may not get a team title, but we will get someone to be an NCAA All-American every year."

"I was always surprised that she didn't leave," Beale said. "She could go anywhere she chose, but she stayed. We were so fortunate she stayed in Lubbock."

To schedule a track meet outside of a ninety-mile radius

Styling despite the surroundings; From left, Athletic Trainer, Sue Rocque and Assistant Coach, Beale Tolbert

patterned a scavenger hunt, but Jarvis succeeded. She wanted the team to embrace her vision of stretching the budget. Once posting the travel roster, an announcement followed.

"I'm not spending all of this money for nothing," Jarvis would say. "We didn't come to play! I'm paying for people who want to make it to the finals!"

Coach Scott also worked to reorganize the travel schedule. While it expanded outside of West Texas, big track meets such as the Kansas Relays, Drake Relays, or Penn Relays weren't on the calendar. Tabbed as the meet "Where the World's Best Athletes Compete," Mt. SAC Relays was an exception. Tickets to ride weren't free. The following is what she wrote to the team on travel:

April 9, 1987 Notice to Track and Field Athletes: The Angelo State Track and Field Invitational is the last meet for those who are looking to qualify for the Mt. SAC meet. By next week, I will review overall performance times and distances, along with contributions to the team, so I can justify driving to the relays.

"Justify driving to the relays ...?"

Yes. While other coaches across the Southwest Conference were making airline reservations, Coach Scott was looking for justification to drive 1,100 miles. But drive is what we did! From Lubbock, Texas, to Walnut, California, Coach Scott piloted the big beige van down the interstate.

Coach Scott never complained about the dismal financial support. She viewed the hardship as an opportunity and countered any negative remark.

"It's all a part of leadership. If you are faithful over the few things, He will add more," she said. "Don't focus on finances. Keep your eyes on the goal."

While the van rides were at times long and arduous, the standard of excellence never changed. She made sure we maintained our focus.

It didn't matter if we were traveling thirty miles down the highway to Wayland Baptist University or 1,100 miles to Walnut, Coach Scott enforced the dress code policy. Meaning, hair rollers, sweats, or any other attire that gave a hint of "long trip" was not allowed. It didn't stop there. When stopping for a meal, Coach Scott would stand and scan the tables to ensure that each of us left a tip. Good or bad service, not leaving a tip was never an option. She did all of that because she wanted us to know that regardless of our plight or position in life, to not lose sight of the goal.

Reading, singing, listening to music, swapping stories, and sleeping on one another—we did it all riding in the beige van. And though our bodies were weary, once we arrived at our destination, we stepped off the van like we had departed the first-class section of an airplane.

It wasn't always easy. We were envious of schools that did not travel by van. But we soon took in the lesson. No matter the "vehicle," do not allow your confidence to be squelched. Keep your eyes on the task at hand. If you keep going, you will arrive at your destination. Although the mode of transportation may seem to be a crawl, walk, or run, we must keep moving forward and move with purpose. If by some chance it is a walk, well ... walk like you are going somewhere.

Leadership Principle #9

Helping team members to maintain focus is the goal of great leaders. They influence others to look beyond what they see. They don't reinforce complaining from team members about what they don't have. Instead, they encourage them to act as though they have it.

While you may not have the supporting cast or the finances to support your efforts, keep going. Stay focused on the task at hand and use what you have!! The impact you make on others will go a lot further than you ever imagined. How? I'm so glad you asked. If you delight in even the small successes, and the present outcome, the people around you are more likely to be motivated and will stay the course with you.

Focus, no matter what's going on around you. Don't allow the noise to distract you.

CHAPTER 10

The Call to Know When and How to Delegate

> *"Although you are the captain of your ship, leading is not a solo trip. Don't just take charge but take others along with you."*—J

New Beginnings

One year after arriving at Texas Tech, Coach Scott set out to make the most of her limited budget. She narrowed her choice of graduate assistants to Jan Chesbro, a recent graduate and high jumper from Texas A&M University. Jan received the call in November of 1980.

While sitting in the hotel room, preparing for the next day's interview, an impromptu knock at the door caught Jan off guard. She opened the door to see Jarvis standing there. Jarvis's eyes lit up.

"I was excited to interview you!"

Jan began her duties the next month.

For Coach Scott, her first hire complemented her strengths and weaknesses. Hiring Jan also provided an opportunity to develop the youngster's skill set. Jan's duties included coaching all the field events as well as helping with driving the van.

Coach Scott assigned her not only coaching all the running events but also assuming administrative and recruiting duties.

"I didn't know anyone that worked as hard," Jan said.

And despite Jan's youth, Coach Scott trusted her to complete the assigned tasks.

"Even though I was very young and inexperienced, she allowed me to do my job. Everyone always knew who was in charge, but there was a great freedom as well," Jan said.

Yet everyone knew that with their role came responsibility. For instance, while on the way to the NCAA Championships, Jan and Mary Johnson, the athletic trainer, weren't mindful of the time. They decided to get something to eat but forgot about the change in the time zone and missed the flight.

"Jarvis was not thrilled the least bit!" Jan said.

We made it to the meet, thanks to Sharon Moultrie. She talked Jarvis out of taking their tickets with her on the plane. Instead, Jarvis left the tickets at the gate.

"It was totally Jarvis!" Jan said.

The new graduate from Aggieland felt nothing but gratitude: "I will never comprehend what made her take a chance on me. There was nothing special about me."

Jan left Texas Tech in 1982, taking her knowledge and skills to Rockport (Texas) High School, followed by the University of Arizona and Baylor University.

Jan Chesbro

"I loved being at Tech, but I hated being in Lubbock," she said.

In the Driver's Seat

Coach Scott's second hire and first full-time coach was Beale Tolbert. The twenty-five-year-old teacher and coach from Gregory Portland (Texas) High School heard from a friend that Jarvis needed an assistant. She knew of Jarvis's Olympic story but nothing of her coaching capabilities. Recognizing that she did not have a similar athletic résumé as Jarvis, she did know West Texas and that she was gifted at recruiting. Moreover, she was determined to outwork others. Beale landed the job at Texas Tech in 1982.

Once again Coach Scott had no problem assigning duties. Beale was responsible for coaching all the field events. Coaching some of the distance runners was added to Beale's list the next year.

Beale didn't possess all the gifts of a distance coach, but she put in the work. It was easier to put forth the effort because Coach Scott trusted Beale. She never changed one workout the twenty-five-year-old wrote.

"I knew she trusted me," Beale said. "It was tremendously important to my professional growth to know that she respected me."

Jarvis spent time teaching Beale about speed development and the mental aspect of overcoming doubt.

"One of the reasons I wanted to work with her was because of our shared belief that you build a track team around a 400," Beale said. "Over my forty-year career, my teams were known for 400- and 800-meter runners, mile relays, and field events."

More so than the shared belief, Jarvis wanted Beale to feel confident in her role as a leader.

In 1983, Jarvis became pregnant. That same year, distance runner Maria Medina qualified for her first NCAA Division I Cross Country Championships, in Lehigh, Pennsylvania. Jarvis was too far along in her pregnancy to travel and therefore had Beale accompany and coach Maria.

"What do you want me to do?" Beale asked.

"Exactly what I would do," Jarvis said.

Unfortunately, while driving to the hotel in Pennsylvania, Beale got turned around. They ended up about a mile away from the Pennsylvania and New Jersey border. Beale pressed to make it to the hotel in enough time to call Jarvis, because she didn't want her to know they got lost. During the call, Jarvis never let on that she knew they got lost.

A week later, while sitting in her office, Beale asked, "Is it going to be a long day?"

Jarvis replied, "It won't be if my assistant gets her directions right."

Beale later said, "We weren't trained to screw up. If you screwed up, you had to own it."

Although Jarvis wasn't impressed with Beale's navigational challenges, she was pleased with the outcome of the cross country meet. Maria placed 67th. And Beale's confidence increased to another level.

Beale Tolbert

"I owe Jarvis so much," she said.

Rising Tide Boats Lift One Another

Teamwork and trust always earmarked Jarvis's coaching, and decisions were well thought out. A formal introduction nor drawn-out explanation parted her lips.

"On Tuesdays and Thursdays, the long and triple jumpers will go with Coach Abe Brown," she said.

I wasn't certain when the decision or discussion between Coach Scott and the men's assistant coach took place. What I did know is giving Coach Brown the duty of coaching the female long and triple jumpers gave no reprieve from hard work.

I dreaded Tuesday workouts. After finishing the warm-up, I walked across the infield and attempted to hype myself for Coach Brown. He stood on the east side of the track and moved alongside the hurdles. Step by step, he placed one foot in front of the other. I didn't have to get much closer to see his lips counting off his steps. One, two, three, four, five. After every five counts, he placed a hurdle. Ten hurdles at a height of forty-eight inches. He stepped back and gazed at the beauty of the symmetry.

"Oh, yeah!" His laugh sounded like an infectious dare.

The hurdle hop drill involved two-legged bounces over ten hurdles, with one hop in between each one. I always found it easier to do a double hop in between, but he didn't allow for shortcuts.

I bit on the inside of my lip and let out an enormous sigh. Coach Brown looked up and greeted me with the usual.

"Banks!" He patted me on the shoulder. The sunbeam bounced off the rings on his fingers. He giggled again and jogged off to the locker room.

When he turned the corner, I took my chances and lowered the hurdles.

Moments later, Coach Brown shouted, "Who moved my hurdles? Banks, did you touch my hurdles?!"

Mission failed. He moved the hurdles back up and stood guard from start to finish. I didn't know if my heart pounded from my chest or my head. My eyes widened watching the other jumpers leap over the hurdles with ease. My stalling tactic flopped.

"Let's go, Banks!" Coach Brown said.

I took a deep breath and approached the hurdles with a confident swagger. I swung both arms and hopped over the hurdles. Dat, dat, dat, dat! Coach Brown leaped with excitement.

"Oh, yeah!" he said.

When I approached the fifth hurdle, I lost my rhythm and guts.

"Baaaanks! C'mon now … use your arms," he said.

Six down, but I had four more sets to complete. Off in the distance, I could feel Coach Scott watching me. It took me longer than everyone else, but Coach Brown made sure I completed every repetition of hurdle hops. Coach Brown's no-excuse policy played like a song on repeat. Big or small, we left no task undone.

A couple of months later, with the wave of one finger, Coach Scott summoned me to the top of the bleachers.

"We've got one week before the conference championships," she said.

The high pitch of my giggle and inability to keep eye contact told her I was nervous.

"You will be just fine."

She stood up and scanned the field. The distance runners ran in a pack.

"Keep it right there!" she yelled.

As they came off the top of the curb, she glanced at her watch. Next, she sat beside me. Pointing at Coach Brown, she said, "I am grateful for Abe. He's the best."

"I am grateful for him too," I said.

And then she imparted words of wisdom. "Never get so high on yourself that you can't ask for help. Iron sharpens iron." She glanced up at the sky. "If you ask Him to send people into your life that can help you develop, He will do it. But don't forget, you must help them develop too."

It was that mind-set that led Jarvis to create some of the men's workouts without ever making it public knowledge. Texas Tech men's sprinter Ronnie Green summarized the partnership: "Jarvis was the architect and Coach Brown was the executor."

Vivid memories of that day in the bleachers are etched in my mind. I often think about how the rule of reciprocity sent ripple effects in my life as well as my teammates'. The rule is the idea of exchanging something with someone in a manner where both people benefit because of mutual respect and communication. Coach Scott had no reservations about enlisting the help of Coach Brown. She knew he produced champions and not chumps and implemented a no-excuse stance. Whether it was those dreaded hurdle hops, box drills, and what appeared to be endless bounding, it was not only to get the best out of his student-athletes, but, like Coach Scott, to teach lasting life lessons.

For instance, because of the limited budget, when I qualified for the Indoor National Championships in Indianapolis in 1988, neither Coach Scott nor Coach Brown could accompany me. Instead, men's head coach Corky Oglesby traveled. I struggled with not having Coach Scott or Coach Brown with me.

Injured during the prelims, I had a disappointing meet. The day after returning from Indianapolis, the three of us stood in the infield of the track. To ease my discomfort, Coach Brown said, "Remember that you will never walk alone."

"Ditto," Coach Scott said.

I left the track encouraged by Coach Brown's reminder but was hoping to hear more than "ditto" from Coach Scott.

Many years later Coach Scott and I stood in her yard and chatted. It was August 2016. I shared the story with Coach Scott of the NCAA 1989 Outdoor Championships in Provo, Utah. It was my last outdoor season. On my third jump during the semifinals, I felt the jolt—the throbbing ran through my hamstring. Saddened that my season was over, I went to the trainer's tent. Before I knew it, Coach Brown was standing over me.

"Banks, what are you doing?" he said.

"I'm hurt," I said.

"Can you walk?" he said.

"Yes. I can walk."

"Well, we have more jumping to do. Let's go."

My eyes screamed.

"Shake it off, Banks. You're not a pansy."

I raised myself off the training table and willed myself into believing the pain was no longer present. The look in Coach Brown's eyes made me believe I could handle the pain. He walked a step behind me as I headed toward the infield of the track.

"I must constantly remind you of the things you already know," he said.

Chill bumps raised up on my arms. Yet, his words stuck. I stepped onto the track and headed for the triple jump runway.

"Banks!" he called out.

I turned around and walked toward him.

He placed his hand on my shoulder and said, "Now is the time to dig deep." He lifted his hand and gave me a high five. And with a big smile that exuded confidence, he began clapping and said, "Baaanks!"

I earned a second-place finish in the triple jump. Coach Brown swooped me up like a proud daddy.

By the time we finished reminiscing, Coach Scott's smile was as bright as the day she met us at the airport. I remember how her smile lit up the terminal. There was no bear hug, but a firm handshake. I knew she was just as proud.

Coach Scott's decision to entrust the jumpers to Coach Brown seemed to make the payoff that much greater. Why? Because in making decisions, worrying about who got the credit never crossed her mind.

Nearly twenty-five years later, the details of the story remained vivid. We laughed and shared a hug. Coach Scott then proceeded toward her house. As she approached the screen door, she paused and said, "Delegating benefits everyone when we get ourselves out of the way."

"Ditto," I said.

Coach Scott chuckled.

Just like that her response from March 1988 came back to me. I then realized Coach Scott responded with "ditto" not only because she agreed but because she had no desire to try and one up Coach Brown.

For those who struggle with asking for help or letting go of doing everything on their own, let this strategy be a reminder. Delegation is an art and can be fully achieved when we are first willing to be vulnerable. Mutual trust was the power tool that drove collaboration and communication between Coach Scott and the other coaches.

Delegating responsibilities is not about turning over the job that you do not want to perform. It is entrusting someone to do the job that you can complete but believe someone can do better.

In those rare instances, you might be able to do the job better than others. In that case, it is about assigning someone a job so that with your guidance and direction, they can gain experience and refine their skills.

Reunited at the 2014 Big 12 Outdoor Championships/Texas Tech Track Reunion; From left: Coach Scott, me, and Coach Brown

Coach Abe Brown

Motivated to move mountains; Me at the 1989 NCAA Outdoor Track and Field Championships in Provo, UT

Leadership Principle #10

Great leaders delegate because they are not worried about who gets the credit. Nor are they worried about their weaknesses getting exposed. Instead, their main concern is ensuring that team members reach collective goals. Regardless of your position, the best leaders recognize that everyone can be commissioned to play an integral role on the team.

The pathway to success is paved with a powerful principle. As the leader, you always have a choice of the route when it comes to a task. You can do it yourself, or you can get someone else to do it for you. Which is it going to be?

CHAPTER 11

The Call to Practice Fairness

> *"When it comes to accountability, there is no all for one and one for all."*—J

No Sweets or Treats

In her one year as a graduate assistant, Jan's observation was spot on about Coach Scott. "She was 100 percent on, every time she stepped on the track."

As she reminisced about the young ladies on the team, Jan quickly added, "Oh my gosh! She cared about every one of those girls! Regardless of who you were, and how good of an athlete, you were hers! She let you know when you were right, and she let you know when you were wrong. She was just matter-of-fact."

Coach Scott didn't have favorites. She simply had girls who in her mind needed different strategies to redirect. Star athlete or walk-on, consequences never ran on empty.

For instance, before continuing to a track meet in Abilene, Texas, the team stopped at a local cafeteria. One by one, the girls grabbed their trays and silverware and placed their requests to the servers.

An array of green and fruit salads filled the front of the buffet line. The cream drizzle on the strawberries and melon screamed, take a bite! As they inched their way down the line, they saw entrée selections, followed by choices of vegetables, and then rolls: wheat, white, or cornbread. Man! To resist the calories.

The decadent aroma of desserts smelled downright sinful. After a quick scan of the line, sprinter Sandra took a slice of a cobbler from the dessert bar. When she got to the table, she shared the cobbler with several of the girls, who delighted in the spoonful of fruit tart.

Chattering and laughter filled the cafeteria. And then the squeal of Coach Scott's chair scooting back sounded an alarm. She began looking around at the tables. After taking a sip of her water, Coach Scott rose from her seat and walked over to the table where Sharon and others sat.

"Who ate the peach cobbler? Somebody had it because it's on the receipt," Jarvis asked.

"She came around looking for it, but we had eaten it," Sharon said.

No one confessed. Silence filled the dining area as customers eavesdropped.

Coach Scott walked back to her table. She pressed her finger on her cheek and shook her head.

After a little over an hour, doors flung open and closed as the girls exited the restaurant. When they got to the van, Coach Scott refused to unlock the door.

"Nobody's getting on the van until we find out who ate the peach cobbler," Jarvis said.

A hush came over the team. The roars of cars and trucks down the highway swallowed the gasps. She commanded the team to jog down the highway until someone confessed.

After running one mile, Coach stopped the van. "Who ate it?"

A struggle to confess weighed like a sandbag.

"Keep running!" she said.

After what they believed to be two miles, she let everyone back in the van.

"We jogged two miles over that spoonful of cobbler!" Sharon exclaimed.

Dump it

We heard the stories about Coach Scott's policies against eating sweets but sheepishly thought the rules didn't apply to long road trips. One morning, we loaded two fifteen-passenger vans and headed for Tempe, Arizona. We didn't know whether to be excited about spring break, leaving the state of Texas, or both. Four hours from our destination, our sweaty skin stuck to the leather seats. Water just would not do, and the heat must have made a few of us delusional.

Coach Scott exited off I-40 and pulled up to a travel center. She exited the van. In usual fashion, intrigue and an unsolved enigma hid behind her mirrored shades as she pumped the gas. Inside the store, we wandered the aisles and chatted as we began grabbing Snickers, chips, and other snacks. I grabbed a honey bun, sour cream and onion potato chips, and a bottle of Gatorade. When the cashier handed the bag to me, my eyes danced at the lip-smacking frosting spread across the roll.

One by one, we paid for our items and headed to the van. As we approached the exit, Jarvis took two steps toward the door.

The passenger screening was quick but painful. When she summoned our bags, she extended her hands with those long fingers and rounded nails.

"Hand over your bags," she said.

She removed the contraband from our bags, handed it back and said, "Dump it."

"Pleeaase!! Can we get our money back?!" I begged.

I didn't need a window to see through her mirrored shades. Her squared shoulders and erect stance said it all. We walked back to the van with heads lowered and eyes rolling. There was no desire to chat. For the next thirty minutes, we stared out the windows, thinking of the snacks she donated.

Jumping the Gun

Coach Scott's syllabus appeared as though it was never void of a lesson.

The kiss of spring made the muddled sound over the loudspeaker sound as clean as the baby blue skies. The Abilene Invitational held in Abilene, TX, was a tune-up prior to the 1986 Outdoor Southwest Conference Championships.

"In lane two, from Texas Tech, Kelly Malacara," the announcer said.

Lined up and ready to run the 200 meters, the starter scanned the field of runners.

"Quiet in the stands," the announcer said.

Coach Scott sat at the top of the stadium wearing her dark, mirrored shades. No wind and no chatter.

"Runners to your blocks," the starter belted.

Before settling in the blocks, runners stretched and kicked their legs out.

"Seettt!" he commanded.

The sprinters' arms were perpendicular to the ground. Their bodies rolled forward into "set" with their heads down.

The starter raised his left arm and pulled the trigger. Bam, bam, bam! Multiple pops of the starter's gun rang out, signaling that someone had either left the blocks early or moved before the gun sounded.

Runners walked back to their blocks. Spectators, athletes, and coaches watched as the starter marched down the lanes to reveal which runner jumped the gun, rendering a disqualification. In a matter of seconds, he picked up Kelly's starting blocks and placed them backwards in her lane.

Coach Scott sprang to her feet. The drumming of her footsteps was ominous as she exited the bleachers. Kelly met her in the infield. What was Coach saying? Did Kelly's blocks slip? Or was she injured?

We followed their every stride. Soon, our attention focused on Kelly as she stood on the other side of the track and on the long jump runway.

"What is she doing?" Georgianna asked.

Coach Scott placed starting blocks on the long jump runway and made Kelly practice coming out of the blocks. Instead of using a starter's gun, Coach Scott clapped her hands as the signal. Creating a state-of-the-art harness with her sweat jacket, each time Kelly shot out of the starting blocks, Coach Scott exerted force with her "harness" to stifle forward motion as Kelly ran. We lost count of the repetitions.

Spectators looked on with jaws dropped and eyebrows raised. While Kelly learned firsthand to never false start again, the rest of us became brilliant students and wise witnesses!

KellyMalacara

The Last Laugh

Her wit evoked both darkness and laughter. So, when she wasn't trying to be funny, you hoped to be the recipient of her effort of laughter. Doris Brown recalled how Jarvis and Barb brought coloring books to help pass the time.

"They just liked to have fun. Before you knew it, others on the team joined in coloring with them," Doris said.

While competing, Jarvis refused to conform, even if she were the oddball. While at the Cross Country Nationals in Idaho, Jarvis could not shake the chill from the thrashing wind and polar air.

Rather than not run, she layered her clothes with the only thing she had available.

"Jarvis ran with her coat on the entire race!" Doris said, chuckling.

"She was a sprinter-type of cross country runner but actually did well," Doris added. "She had a great attitude and was a wonderful sport."

Can laughing be a sign of fear? Funny or not, we knew when to laugh.

Like the women's track team, Corky had a small budget. Whether selling candy bars or approaching potential donors, he made it work. Corky's reputation for coaching track did not precede him, but he excelled in recruiting athletes to Texas Tech. The best.

Whether it was basketball or track, Corky not only recognized top talent but had the ability to convince young men everywhere to come to West Texas. All this from a man who stood no taller than 5 feet 6 wearing a toupee. No one could match the stride of his brisk walking pace. Still, he had difficulty disciplining the strong-willed guys.

But Jarvis possessed a village mind-set.

Coach Scott and Corky collaborated on an idea to give the coaches a break from driving the vans. In the spring of 1987, the men and women boarded a charter bus. The first stop was Albuquerque for an invitational meet. At the end of the meet, we boarded the bus and headed to El Paso for UTEP's Olympian Meet. We were moving up!

Two hours into the trip, one of the top sprinters, Mark, began cracking jokes. He threatened to take up a collection in return for taking off Corky's toupee. Mark never took it that far, but the jokes continued. Some jokes were funny, but the ladies knew not to laugh or become part of the clatter. Next, he began making noises that sounded like a cross between a parrot and a sperm whale. Corky asked Mark to quiet down several times, to no avail.

Coach Scott, Corky, and Coach Brown sat near the front. The bus driver peered through his rearview mirror and rubbed his eyebrow.

Suddenly, Coach Scott rose from her seat and made her way through the bus. Her slender body jostled back and forth. To keep her balance, her hands grabbed the back of seats. The white tape was in her hand. She never uttered a word. No one knew her next move or dared to ask.

Sitting at the back of the bus, Mark did not understand Coach Scott was coming to visit him.

Coach Scott stood in front of Mark and ripped the first piece of tape. Setting the roll under her arm, she placed the strip over his mouth. Next, she took the roll from under her arm, placed her left hand on the top of his head, and with a round and round motion, she began taping Mark's mouth shut. Silence hovered over the entire bus.

If the rearview mirror could talk, the driver's smirk screamed payback.

Texas Tech University Head Men's Track and Field Coach, Gerald "Corky" Oglesby

Texas Tech University Assistant Men's Track and Field Coach, Abe Brown

Texas Tech University Head Women's Track and Field Coach, Jarvis Scott

The Do-over

Coach Scott always found unfamiliar spots for a workout.

One time was in the spring of 1987. Although it was a Monday, we piled in the van. We thought we were certain about our workout destination. As she began to drive east, we whispered to one another, "Mae Simmons." But as she drove further east down 19th Street, Mae Simmons Park was in our rearview mirror.

Located approximately 10 miles southeast of Lubbock, we were certain Buffalo Springs Lake was the destination.

"Oh! Buffalo!" we mouthed.

Nope! We soon found ourselves far out on East 4th Street, approximately 15 miles from Texas Tech.

The van suddenly began to slow. There was nothing around us but a few small houses out in the distance. After coming to a stop, she said, "OK ... here we go. Let's get started."

Flabbergasted by her directive, we slowly exited the van. Mumbling at a volume only we could hear, we huffed and grumbled.

Once everyone exited the van, she said, "Meet me at Mae Simmons."

Fresh off an injury, the thought of running what appeared to be ten miles seemed impossible to me.

As we started to jog, we went back and forth, talking smack about how crazy she was to drop us off in the middle of nowhere. Further along in the run, my legs began to ache, and my pace slowed. Some of my teammates began to look smaller and smaller as they forged ahead. Those of us left behind began to walk.

The van approached us from behind. Her warning was loud and clear: "If I see you walk again, I am going to take you back to the start."

Even though we could no longer see the start, Mae Simmons was nowhere in sight!

Our legs felt like wet spaghetti noodles. We needed a rescue, but relief was a distant wish away. Looking around to see if we could spot her, we tried to sneak a walk in here and there. Before we knew it, like a scene out of *Jeepers Creepers*, the big beige van reappeared.

"Get in the van," she said.

Knots began to fill my stomach. Riding back to the start, my palms began sweating because I didn't know if or how I would make it. But it was my lucky day. As she stopped at the start, she made everyone get out of the van except for me. It wasn't because I was special, but because I was fresh off an injury.

Driving down East 4th Street, I sat quietly and gave thanks to God that I wasn't a part of the group in my rearview mirror. The van moved at a slow pace and the ticking of the caution lights sounded more like a time bomb. Leaning forward, she turned down the radio and looked out the rearview mirror. The rebuke given to my teammates said it all. Accountability must abound in us all. Own up to your actions. If not, they may require reigniting.

Run Past the Finish

Secrets and stories that lurked behind that ugly green fence at our track were too many to count. Regardless of coaching practically every event, Jarvis' placement on or off the field never prevented her from seeing the end of our run.

Once again, during a spring workout in 1988, Coach Scott sat at the top of the stadium wearing her shades. X-ray vision activated as encouragement and threats echoed across the field.

"Use your arms! Lift your knees, lift your knees! Finish strong! Run past the finish line! Finish the race!" echoed across the track and over that hideous green fence.

I prepared for the Monday workout. Six 300s. Starting at the top of the first curve, runners ran three-quarters of one lap.

But now I had to overcome the triple threat. The brown dust and West Texas wind at our backs and the shining marigold orange sun bore down on our skin. A headwind welcomed me on the last 100 meters. The sweat rolled down my face and the taste of salt didn't give a drop of moisture. It parched my mouth. I was nearing the end of a grueling workout. After the fifth 300 meters, I crossed the finish line, bent over, and placed my hands on my knees. I needed a quick rest.

Out of nowhere, I heard the command: "Get up!"

I knew my rest period had not expired and wondered why I was being reprimanded. It was the second and final warning that made me realize I had slowed up at the finish line. My eyes widened at the command.

"Banks, get off your knees and get ready."

Coach didn't yell. Nor did she have to repeat herself.

I rolled my eyes and clenched my jaws so tight I could sense the tension in every muscle. As mad as I was, I wasn't bold enough to defy the directive. Placing my hands on the top of my head, I took a deep breath and walked to the starting line.

She warned, "Don't stop until I tell you!"

It happened so fast, but I could see the red faces of some of my teammates. Whether it was an embarrassment for me or fear of her, no one made eye contact.

Convinced I would pass out, my mind started preparing my body for a stretcher. The upper 80-degree temperature converted to a fiery furnace. I inched up to the start, wiped the sweat from my brow, and listened for the directive: "Go!"

I came around the backstretch. The relentless heat on my arms and the wind whipping in my face would not let up. My stride shortened as I slowed; my breathing quickened. I tried to inhale through my nose and exhale through my mouth. But my throat stung and felt as dry as the West Texas air. I longed for a drop of water.

The cramping in my legs no longer mattered as I headed toward the finish line. All I wanted was to finish. I gathered myself and ran past the pain. Six strides past the finish line, I heard the command.

"Stop!" she yelled.

The consequence did not render me safe from the rest of the workout. I started my sixth 300 four minutes later. When practice ended, she walked over to the infield. I could not see her eyes behind the shades, but the matter-of-fact tone in her voice was evident.

"No race is complete if you don't run past the finish line."

Coach Scott was tough, but she was fair. There wasn't any consequence handed down to us just for the sake of it. More importantly, regardless of the consequence, we knew she cared. Though at times the disciplining seemed harsh, we always knew she was pushing us to be our best. That push motivated us to do better. Not only that, we also knew there was a lesson behind the correction.

From the moment we had to dump our snacks, we learned to eat with intention, or face consequences. When our mouth moved faster than our brain, it was inevitable. We slipped up. The only treat given to us for consideration included this: Train your brain the same way you train your body.

On the bus, it was evident the lesson stuck with everyone, male and female alike. Trainers' tape can cover a multitude of aches and pains.

Even while sitting in the bleachers watching Kelly, we reflected on the message. Nerves will cause you to react rather than respond. When emotions are high and your heart is racing, be intentional with managing your thoughts and responses. No matter what's going on around you, learn to control your reactions, or your reactions will soon control you.

And as I think about that hot dusty day running the 300s, I am reminded to never stop short of the finish line.

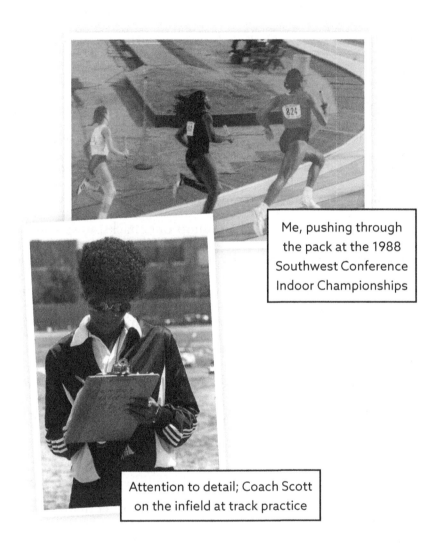

Me, pushing through the pack at the 1988 Southwest Conference Indoor Championships

Attention to detail; Coach Scott on the infield at track practice

Leadership Principle #11

Great leaders create a culture of fairness. They hold everyone accountable for the choices they make. Leaders who demonstrate fairness are consistent with expressing clear-cut expectations. And when the expectations are not met, the consequences are not cookie-cutter or an all-for-one-and-one-for-all approach. Rather, they are unique to the individual and the situation.

As you think about disciplinary actions for your team, are you fair or are you fickle? Only one will empower your team. Promote a climate where everyone is mindful of the standards and rules, and ultimately promote change.

CHAPTER 12

The Call to Build on Lessons from the Past

> *"We know too little of the trials and victories of those who have gone before us. May we diligently study their lives to glean a storehouse of knowledge. I ask this in the all holy name of the Father, Son, and Holy Spirit."—J*

Don't Forget to Remember

"Where are the hills?"

When Coach Scott first arrived in Lubbock, a location to run on an incline was fresh on her mind.

Mae Simmons Park was the second-best location for Coach Scott. She created some of the fiercest workouts at that park. She called one of the hardest workouts Max. A high-intensity interval workout for middle-distance and long-distance runners, they would have to run 300 meters up hill, jog down for a short 50 meters, and then do continuous sprints up hill. Whatever the variation—up, down, across, up, down, up, down, across and over—would make up one Max! For sprinters, there would be 100-, 200-, or 300-meter sprints up the hill. If the area were large enough, Coach Scott would have made a 400-meter straight out of it.

I never ran a Max. Instead, Coach Scott relied on Coach Brown to unleash his fury. Mae Simmons was one spot he would express his principle. Every workout at the park began with a two-mile warm-up.

We started the warm-up at the goal post and jogged the first 200 meters on a straightaway. A steep incline a little past the 200-meter mark stretched a scant distance but challenged runners. I was getting close to the one-mile mark but had to conquer the ascent. Gasping for air, I kept my pace steady.

"Banks, don't let me catch you!"

The cars driving north and south down Quirt Avenue helped block out his challenge. I picked up my speed and continued to jog. Yet the jangling of the keys in his pocket was now like cymbals clashing. As he ran past me, he laughed.

"I told you not to let me catch you."

After I finished the workout, Coach Scott sat next to me. "He didn't catch you just because he could. He caught you because you had already decided the challenge was too much."

I raised my eyebrows.

"Tiger. What do you know about Mae Simmons?" Coach Scott asked.

"It gives me nightmares. That's all I know," I said.

Chuckling, she said, "No, Tiger. What do you know about Mae Simmons? The woman."

"Nothing," I replied.

"Before you come back to the park, I want you to find out and let me know," she said.

Two days later, I went to her office to share my lesson about Mrs. Mae Simmons. A former principal and teacher, she was also a civic leader and community advocate for almost thirty years in East Lubbock.

Coach Scott rose from her chair and walked over to the window. The view was perfect for a Red Raider football game, but there was something about the way she looked. Narrow and immovable.

"Mae Simmons was also a granddaughter of slaves." Her stare held the football field hostage, and it seemed she had left on a journey into the quest for equity in education.

"If you think she didn't have obstacles, Tiger, think again. Getting a master's degree in the 1940s for a black woman was difficult. You all are fortunate to get an education, without the hardships that those before you experienced. You might have nightmares from the workouts, but that will only be temporary."

She walked back to her desk and pushed the papers aside. "Remember this—I never want you to face a mountain without having assurance that you can conquer it. You will make it to the top, but do not forget there are two parts. Once you climb, don't underestimate the value in going back down."

She patted me on my shoulder and said, "Thanks, Tiger! Now, don't be late to practice. We have hills today."

I thought she was trying to give a lesson on downhill training.

Before I reached the door, she said, "Hold on, Tiger." When I turned around, she was holding an envelope.

"Here. Look," she said.

Dated March 1976, the return address said, "Mickey's Missile." I opened the envelope and began to read the card.

"Have you heard of Mickey?" she said.

I placed the card in the envelope, handed it back and said, "No."

As she strummed her fingers across the envelope, Coach Scott said, "I was in rare air."

In the early 1970s, Jarvis met Mickey Patterson-Tyler, the first black woman to win an Olympic medal. Sharing space with her humbled Jarvis. Patterson-Tyler placed third in the 200 at the 1948 Olympics held in London. Sadly, New Orleans, the city she loved, failed to honor her. The mayor at that time did not attend a ceremony in her honor, and *The Times-Picayune* local newspaper failed to identify Patterson as a hometown girl.[14]

Mickey fought back. Shortly after graduating from Southern University, the bronze medalist moved to San Diego, and in 1965, she organized Mickey's Missiles, a track club initially for girls. The club would soon admit boys.

Placing the envelope on her desk, Coach Scott said, "Challenges will come, but you have to persevere. You might be tempted to ease up or stop. There will be those who don't acknowledge your contributions. No matter what comes your way, be like Mickey and condition your mind to ignore false signs of fatigue and continue at maximum."

Jarvis was able to ignore the signs because she always remembered Mickey's admonishment. "When your legs feel like they are giving out, run with your heart."

Years later we sat in Coach's living room. She handed me another envelope.

"Look at this, Tiger," she said.

Inside was a letter of congratulations on Coach Scott's induction into the 2017 Hall of Fame–California Interscholastic Federation (CIF) Los Angeles City Section.

A gust of excitement overtook me. "Wow!"

Her face was devoid of any emotion.

"Did you read it?" I asked her.

"Yes. I read it."

Rendered speechless, a response escaped me. After a brief silence, she said, "My time is up. I just want to sit back and experience the joy of the recognitions for the hard work and accomplishments of you all."

Her eyes gleamed with pride as she began rattling off names and accomplishments of former student-athletes.

No surprise. She made her accolades about everyone else.

Moments later, she brandished an envelope.

"Mickey," she said. I leaned in and said, "Ma'am?"

Her eyes stared boldly at me. "Don't forget," she said.

She pulled the letter out of the envelope and said, "I didn't make it on my own. I will never forget that anything I face is an obstacle that someone has already conquered." The letter read as follows:

March 4, 1976
Dear Jarvis,
I am getting ready for the FREEDOM GAMES to be held in San Diego at Balboa Stadium on May 15, 1976. Competition from all over the nation will be here. I already have a confirmation from Debra Sapenter from Texas. Jarvis, you know I have been in your corner all the time; you are one of my favorites. I especially want you to be a part of the Games. I hope you have been working hard. Cynthia should be able to hold her own in the Junior Division. I won't expose her to the Senior Division yet. She is fifteen now, so she has plenty of time. I hope you will be able to come to San Diego, possibly the night before the meet. I will be happy to make arrangements for your lodging and meals. I have a lot to tell you when I see you again. If for any reason you

cannot attend, would you send me a picture and résumé, if you do decide to come for publicity purpose as well? Some people here would like you to be on a television show that will be taped on March 29th. I will be talking to you more about this soon. I am looking forward to hearing from you. Please forward the résumé and picture as soon as possible and let me know of your plans, so that we can get everything together here.

Yours in Sports,

Sincerely,

Audrey "Mickey" Tyler

P.S. Jarvis, would you be able to meet with me, Johna Cole, Channel 10, Wyomia Tyus, and Barb Ferrell in Los Angeles, next Thursday, March 11, at 1:00 p.m.? Would you call me and suggest a good meeting place?

P.P.S. Jarvis, would you give me Barb Ferrell's phone number and address? Also, I need Wyomia Tyus's phone number and address. I did have them, but somehow misplaced them.

May 1976

Shortly after the Freedom Games, Jarvis received a thank you card from Coach Mickey.

Dear Jarvis,
The meet was a tremendous success. I would like to express my deepest appreciation to you and the other girls for coming to San Diego and competing in our meet, thereby giving the children

the chance to see world-class athletes in action. Good luck in the Olympic Trials.

With warm regards,

Mickey Tyler

1948 U.S. Olympic Team photo

Founder of Mickey's Missile Track Club, 1948 Olympian, Audrey "Mickey" Patterson

Reminiscing on Mickey Patterson-Tyler's letter, I thought, whether your cheering section is on earth or on high, remember that your blood, sweat, and tears are a little lighter because someone wanted to provide you with better.

Skeeter

Jarvis also carried the lessons learned from her childhood hero. As a twelve-year-old, Jarvis watched Wilma Rudolph line up in lane three to run the 100-meter dash at the 1960 Rome Olympics. Her eyes glued on the black-and-white television with foil fixed on the antenna. Wilma Rudolph, nicknamed "Skeeter" for her speed, would win three gold medals and set three Olympic records.

As much as she loved watching her hero run, Jarvis admired Wilma's determination and grit. Wilma wore leg braces until the age of nine, because of a bout of scarlet fever followed by pneumonia and polio. Doctors said she'd never walk.

Wilma Rudolph also experienced the ugliness of segregation in the south.

Jumping ahead ... it was eleven days into one of the hottest of months, July 2011. Standing in Coach Scott's backyard in Texas, cotton balls that resembled the Michelin man drifting in and out of our vision filled the sky. Not too far away, the neighbor's lawn mower roared. When she picked up her cane, Coach Scott tilted her head and motioned me to follow her.

She took me around to explain the significant piles displayed throughout the lawn. What looked like chaos turned out to be a methodical system. A section existed for Cooper, her Chihuahua, and a corner section for recyclables. There was also a section where she taught athletes how to use starting blocks. To the west of her wooden fence sat two rusted sets of Newton starting blocks. She leaned over and turned the block upwards.

"It still works," she said.

Next, Jarvis pointed to a small garden bordered with rocks. Hues were white, gray, red, and black. To the naked eye, the garden did not have any special qualities. She laid her cane on the ground, knelt, and began pulling weeds.

"Isn't it amazing how He can make something beautiful out of something so ugly?"

She relished the moments of seeing any flower or plant bloom. Pointing at the sectioned area, she said, "Skeeter ... that's what I call my garden ... Skeeter."

It took effort to see the beauty in the half-bloomed flowers.

"Lessons I learned from gardening are constant reminders that I learned from Skeeter. You will encounter some weeds and little critters but decide that you won't allow them to choke you out," she said.

"Understood," I said.

We walked back inside. Coach Scott stood at the screen door and gazed at her backyard.

"Study and learn from those who came before you. Believe me, you will be glad you did," she said in a whisper.

Wisdom and emotion resounded in every word. She made her way to the living room and pointed at the picture of her and Wilma Rudolph.

My jaw dropped. How did I miss this?

She laughed. "Let me show you something else," she said.

My mouth was agape, looking at the picture of former Texas Tech University long-distance runner Maria Medina standing next to Wilma Rudolph.

"I wish all of you could have met her," she said.

"How did Maria get so lucky?" I asked.

"We were in Indianapolis. I told Maria we would spend the rest of the day with someone."

Jarvis sipped on her Pepsi and continued the story.

"Maria didn't want to go. She asked if she could stay at the hotel. I told her, 'No. You will enjoy it.'"

Thirty minutes later, Maria stood motionless in front of one of the greatest athletes of all time. She grabbed the sides of her head and let out a shriek. Maria beamed at the special moment as she took in the stories Jarvis and Wilma exchanged.

"It was not only like watching two schoolgirls but it was like a history lesson unfolding," Jarvis said.

As I held the picture in my hand, Jarvis shared another gardening lesson—there were times when nothing would grow in her garden.

"Not even weeds," she said.

"What made you continue to garden?" I asked.

"I had to believe the seeds I planted would grow even though I couldn't see them."

Just when I had taken it all in, Coach Scott leaned forward and said, "No garden will ever thrive without deposits."

What a valuable lesson I learned that day standing at the garden. I began to think about the Mae Simmons homework assignment as well as previous stories about Mickey Patterson-Tyler and Wilma

Rudolph. All along Coach Scott was trying to create a culture wherein contributions of those who most would deem as trailblazers were recognized.

Why? Because she recognized that she reaped the benefits of those who came before her. No matter how many times her name was printed in the newspaper or the number of awards she amassed, Coach Scott knew that she didn't arrive on her own.

Coach Scott's willingness to sit at the feet of wise leaders imparted insight beyond her years. It also showed her how to demonstrate courage in the face of adversity. On several occasions she humbly declared that her path being less rocky was not because of her own merit.

Wilma Rudolph, 1960 Olympic Team photo.

Maria Medina and Wilma Rudolph (Indianapolis, 1986)

Mentoring matters; 3-time gold medalist (1960 Olympics) Wilma Rudolph and Jarvis

Leadership Principle #12

Let Coach Scott's declaration be a model for you. First, great leaders acknowledge there is no such thing as being self-made. For that reason, they respect and recognize those who came before them as a source of wisdom.

Great leaders remain teachable. They do this by learning what others before them have done and how they handled similar situations. You can never stop learning. Allow history to teach you by nurturing relationships with other leaders. It will help you to understand your position and navigate problems.

Additionally, great leaders are not driven by attention or applause. As such, résumés or accomplishments do not have to define you as leader, but they can certainly develop you. That is, if you allow it. Even better, let it ignite your gratitude. Regardless of your current position or rank, you ... yes, you ... are standing on someone's shoulders. Once you acknowledge those who have preceded you, don't rob them of their success. Winning or losing, as you travel down the highway of life, leadership is up to you. Whose shoulders do you stand on?

CHAPTER 13

The Call to Empathize

> *"I'd rather wake up each day and say that I did everything in my power to save a life, than to say, 'To each his own.'"*—J

The Struggle

Coach Scott didn't need to see Katie's bruises because she had an innate ability to sense trouble. Vivid details leading up to that day were carved in her memory bank. Mike, Katie's boyfriend, objected to Katie hanging out with her friends. If watching track practice was a spectator sport, he'd win the MVP award. Of Goliath proportions, his arms bulged like an unlawful weapon. And his insecurities fueled when guys spoke to Katie. Fire spit from the stadium.

Soon, Katie began tweaking the workout. Somewhere between

the fifth and sixth 200, she'd visit the ladies' room, never to return to finish the eight 200s.

Two days later, Katie missed practice. News of Katie staying in a motel with Mike troubled Coach Scott. She enlisted Corky to help devise a plan.

"Enough is enough."

"Well, what do you want me to do?" he said.

"Either I will go to jail, or somebody better go get her."

The two agreed on a strategy. "Corky enlisted one of the guys to get Mike out of the motel," she said.

Moments later, Coach Scott drove into the motel parking lot. The familiar scene provided reassurance of the exit plan. Prostitution and drug deals were a common fixture at the motel. Before Jarvis could open the door, a BMW pulled up. A woman strolled to the passenger window and then entered the car. Nearby, men exchanged handshakes like passing hot potatoes. The window in the quaint office had a view of all the rooms. Uncertain if Mike was gone, Coach Scott marched into the office and requested the manager to call the room. Moments later, Yvette knocked on the door, and Katie walked out of the guest room.

As Coach Scott drove away, Katie's shoulders sunk, and her body collapsed in the passenger's seat. The emotional scars were raw.

After a brief silence, Katie said, "Thank you."

When Mike asked Katie to move into the motel with him,

she felt like the luckiest girl on the campus. But gradually, Mike's behavior became more controlling.

"He told me I couldn't go to practice. I didn't know what to do," Katie said.

"You don't have to explain," Coach Scott said. And like a babbling brook, Katie continued.

"He kept calling the room to make sure I hadn't left. I didn't know what to do. I wanted to go to practice. I really did. Please believe me."

"I believe you," Coach Scott said.

Katie buried her face in her hands and began to wail. The sound of Katie's sob hit Coach Scott and Yvette in the chest. Coach Scott laid her hand on Katie's leg and said, "I'm here."

And as she promised our parents, Coach Scott was always present. Thirty years later, we sat in her living room and swapped stories. She leaned over and picked up a pendant from underneath the newspaper. As she held it up, the ray of sunshine caused the wing of the butterfly to sparkle.

"All of you young ladies were in cocoons, but it was my responsibility to not stunt your growth," she said. "Where was I?"

On to another story. One in which I already knew the horrid details.

It was a Saturday night, and several of us hung out in my dorm room. Laughter and chatter filled the room as we watched the American Music Awards.

Suddenly, there was a knock on the door.

"Hey there, Allison, Gary is in your room."

"How did he get in my room?"

"I thought you wanted me to let him in," Mary said.

Mary had no idea that Allison broke up with Gary months prior. Already in a dating relationship, Allison wondered why Gary showed up without notice, let alone an invitation.

When Allison entered her room she said, "What are you doing here?"

"Nice to see you too," he said.

"What are you doing here? I told you ... we are finished."

His stare was as intense as his declaration. Walking toward her he said, "I will show you who's best for you."

It happened so fast ...

The force of his body pushing up against her caused the bed to catch her fall.

"I panicked and couldn't even yell," she said.

When Gary pulled up his pants, he said, "What else do I have to do to prove my love?" He walked out as though he had prepared a candlelit dinner.

One month later the pregnancy test confirmed her fear. "I didn't want to lose my scholarship, and I didn't want to disappoint Jarvis.

What would I tell my parents? I didn't want to disappoint them or my grandparents?" she said.

She walked into Coach Scott's office and told her the story.

"I will support you with whatever decision you make," Jarvis said.

Once again, she used her struggles to aid others through the hollow darkness.

Jarvis's ability to empathize ignited a longing to reduce others' pain or stress. Walking in someone's shoes was not enough. She wanted to leave the shoes in better condition, and the only way to do that was to act.

Ronnie Green was a transfer sprinter from Eastern New Mexico University in Portales, New Mexico. During Ronnie's junior year at Texas Tech, his girlfriend became pregnant. Coupled with his parents divorcing, Ronnie was at a crossroad. He found comfort and compassion in daily phone calls from Jarvis. Although conversations never took place during track practice, Ronnie knew Jarvis's words would never fail him.

"She kept me mentally stable," he said.

The guidance and wisdom she provided left an indelible mark on Ronnie.

"While everyone else flew at 10,000–15,000 feet, Jarvis was at 50,000 feet. She flew with the eagles," he said.

Ronnie was not the only male recipient of Coach Scott's display of empathy. She found calming yet creative ways to respond to the needs of others. One such recipient was Leonard Harrison, a 100- and 200-meter runner, who was born and raised in Dallas and was set to graduate from Texas Tech in December of 1987.

"What do you want to do when you graduate?" Jarvis asked.

"Get a job and go back home," he answered.

"Is that what you really want to do?"

Leonard hesitated, and then said, "No, not really. I would like to train for the '88 Olympics."

Coach Scott went on to say that she had seen his hard work and dedication throughout the years and wanted to help him train for the 1988 Olympics. Her counter was simple.

"Let's train. You are now Premier Track Club," she said. "I will foot the bill."

From that day, Leonard began training with Jarvis. "She offered me a chance to achieve my goal," he said.

While standing in the infield of R. P. Fuller Track, she said, "I have already picked the colors. I just need your sizes. By the first meet, you'll be ready."

When I think about various stories and struggles, I am filled with awe at how Coach Scott was able to master responding with empathy and compassion. She had an innate ability to pay attention to nonverbal cues as much as verbal cues. Regardless of the smiles on our face, or pep in our step, she was mindful to look for signs of stress, pain, or discomfort.

Because Coach Scott was focused on people and not the product, it was easier for her to recognize problems. Regardless of gender, race, sexual orientation, or religion, rather than overlook difficulties team members might be experiencing, she put love in action. Because she possessed a heart for people, she refused to be a bystander.

Proof that women coaches matter;
Above: All-American sprinter, Ronnie
Green; Below: Sprinter, Leonard Harrison

Leadership Principle #13

Great leadership is a matter of the heart. When you lead with your heart rather than your head, it becomes difficult to negate the power of being present. Great leaders will feel pain when you feel pain, even if they never utter a word. The needs of great leaders become secondary, because making a difference in someone's life is all that matters.

Leaders who demonstrate empathy in turn empower their team to make it through challenging circumstances. Connections are also made that result in stronger relationships and improved productivity.

After the Creator, empathic leadership is putting others second and self last. In essence, you fully understand—investing in others is up to you, but it's not about you!

Go and do likewise!

CHAPTER 14

The Call to Create Teachable Moments

> *"My grandmother used to tell me I was an old soul. I always had an awareness, but before I could continue to learn and develop, I had to be willing to listen to the lesson."—J*

Press Toward the Mark

Coach Scott's favorite workout spot was Buffalo Springs Lake. No location within at least a sixty-mile radius of Lubbock had steeper hills. Determined to build our strength and stamina by running hills, the entry fee did not deter her. Before arriving at the entry gate, we ducked down on the floor of the van so the entrance fee would not be as steep. Boy! I wish they had charged the full price. Perhaps that would have been a deterrent. But the joke was on us.

"Hi, Coach," the attendant said.

It was as though he knew we were coming and was gracious enough to not charge extra.

The heat bounced off the pavement and straight through the soles of my tennis shoes. The workout was eight 150 meters, with a jog in between. Coach Scott drove the creepy beige Texas Tech van behind us. The radio blasted, but the moaning, mumbling, and heavy panting sang to another beat. I had to be somewhere on about the fifth 150-meter hill. I wondered if I would live to see another hill.

My run up the hill turned into a jog and then into a crawl. The bumper was soon on my tail.

"Get up, Banks! I will hit you!" Coach Scott said.

As tired and worn out as I was, getting hit sounded like a suitable option compared to running another hill. My hands pressed on the hot pavement, and it took everything to stand and finish the hill. With my head held down, I snuck a peek to see her location.

"Don't look back!" she yelled out.

While on the last 150, my legs cried out for relief as I gasped for air. I ignored the admonishment and looked back again.

After cooling down and stretching, I agonized about the rubdown from Coach Scott. Also, the fear of a delayed punishment heightened my worry. Her thumbs gliding along my quadriceps made me want to holler. How could the pressure decrease muscle tension, let alone ease pain?

"Breathe," she said.

After a brief pause, she left me speechless. "Looking back will only cause you to drift. Keep your eyes on the path."

Mental Strength Training

Perhaps it was her view of transferable skills that motivated Coach Scott to aid student-athletes in reaching their full potential.

"I want you all to be ready for the world. I am going to do as your mama would have me to do," she said.

To be ready, Coach Scott believed that sports served as a vehicle for us to learn to compete against ourselves more than others.

"You must learn to be competitive regardless of challenges," she said.

Day in and day out, a key ingredient for Coach Scott included mental toughness. She possessed an uncanny ability to control her emotions and keep a sense of peace, regardless of what was going on around her. It is conceivable she learned to make that tool an art form early on when hell was breaking loose. More than any athletic ability, she knew that mental toughness played a major role in achieving goals on and off the track. And Coach Scott recruited student-athletes whom she could teach and develop that same mind-set.

Coach Scott would say, "You might fail, but it doesn't matter as long as you have a fight in you. To those who never try, you will never feel empowered or a sense of self-confidence. There is victory in every minor achievement, just for trying. The start begins with believing."

I believe one of the best students in Coach Scott's classroom was Aimee Sue Frescaz. A hurdler, Aimee was working at the Burger Kitchen in Levelland, Texas, about thirty miles west of Lubbock, when she got the call from Jarvis.

"Hi, this is Jarvis Scott, the head track coach at Texas Tech." Aimee's mouth dropped. "I'd like to offer you a full scholarship."

Aimee liked the offer but had committed to attending the University of Texas El Paso. Although she needed time to think and knew nothing about Coach Scott, the distance of both universities to home broke the tie. Levelland thirty miles, El Paso three hundred miles.

I sat in the stadium and watched with amazement as Aimee stepped on the track at meets. When she lined up against competitors, her body language told the story. She believed like the shepherd David she could slay any giant. Like a reigning champion, she never flinched. Neither was she bothered that she lost the last race, or the race before. For Aimee, the last tape-breaking moment occurred in high school. But the lessons on having fortitude and fearlessness were etched in her mind.

Aimee persevered and endured, having three coaches in four years. Coach Scott was her first but retired at the end of Aimee's freshman year.

"She sat us down and told us she was getting older and wanted to spend time with her son," Aimee recalled.

Aimee relied on tools taught by Coach Scott. For example, she learned that self-confidence was key. She also learned that regardless of her position in life, take pride in everything and stand by her decisions and actions.

"I had her for one year, but she affected my entire life. I never won a race, but I won because I had her," Aimee said. "She provided me with something in my life that no one else will ever give me. I had her for one year, and that was enough."

Performance was no doubt important to Coach Scott, but learning was even more paramount with mastery of goals. "Some people spend more time and energy gaining strength than seeking mastery of the sport itself," she said.

Even though Aimee never won a race, she never focused on her losses. Instead, she learned from the best. She learned to bounce back and to not lose the fight or faith.

Building confidence one barrier at a time. Hurdler, Aimee Sue Frescaz

Sisterly Love

Years later, Coach Scott's path seemed to be filled with recognition long overdue. The second honor in two years, Coach Scott was to receive a Lifetime Service Award. As we sat in her living room, two of the five televisions remained turned on, a replay of the 2009 presidential inauguration of Barak Obama on one, and a segment about the anniversary of the federal holiday honoring Dr. Martin Luther King Jr. on another.

When I handed Coach Scott the gift bag from my mom, her eyes lit up. Tilting her head, she said, "Very nice ... she knows what I like."

The next evening, we drove to the Overton Conference Center in Lubbock. Laughter filled the back seat, as my mom and Coach

Scott swapped stories from my undergraduate years. My jaw dropped hearing some of their stories, but I relished that the two of them shared a genuine relationship.

Moments later, I pulled up to the front entrance of the hotel. As my mom walked around to help Coach out of the car, she leaned forward and grabbed my shoulder.

"31:28, Tiger," she said.

Uncertain of what she was talking about, I said, "Ma'am?"

"31:28," she said.

"OK ... yes, ma'am."

I had no idea what she was talking about, but the momentous occasion made every moment memorable. Waiting to greet Coach Scott, former athletes stood in the lobby: Louise, Dora, Sharon, Georgianna, and Cheryl. As we stopped to take a group picture, hugs, laughter, and chatter filled the air. Many had not seen one another, or Coach Scott, in years. And through the chatter I could hear Coach Scott ask two questions of her former student-athletes and even some friends.

"How are the children doing? How is your mom doing?"

I don't know if she had met every parent of all her student-athletes, but she often reminded us we were reflections of our mothers.

After taking pictures we entered the banquet hall and sat at the table designated for the honorees. There was no seating arrangement other than Coach Scott's request that my mom sit at her table.

"Edna, I would be honored for you to sit at this table," she said.

"OK, baby," my mom said.

The night went on and Coach Scott received her honor. It did not matter that many in the room were hearing accolades about Lubbock's best-kept secret for the first time. What mattered were moments spent with those she loved and those who loved her more.

At the end of the dinner, we took pictures, conversed with many in the room, and then headed home. Coach Scott began thanking my mom for her gift. The two then continued reminiscing. When we arrived at Coach Scott's house, we exchanged hugs and good-byes. And before closing the car door, she looked at me and spoke one word.

"Proverbs."

The next morning Coach Scott called to say thank you. After expressing her gratitude, she said, "Mothers are special. Mine is no longer here, but I still call her blessed." Her voice quivered. She paused for a moment and then said, "Your mother is special. Never forget that, Tiger."

Once again, Coach Scott's expressions and reminder helped to put things in perspective. Proverbs 31:28: "Her children rise up and call her blessed."

And before hanging up the phone she said, "No other person can ever give birth to you or carry you in her womb. Mothers give life."

Sister friends;
Mama and Jarvis

Celebrating Coach Scott's Lifetime
Achievement Award bestowed by the
100 Black Men of West Texas on January
21, 2017; From left: Louise Hudson, Dora
Bentancourt-Scott, Sharon Moultrie-Bruner,
Georgianna Jones-Hallman, Cheryl Young-Lewis

The Light of Her Life

Coach Scott gave birth to a boy weighing five pounds, twelve ounces. Born on November 15, 1983, Shaun Christopher Scott-Jones was the light of Jarvis's life. With long eyelashes, he was a spitting image of his mother. Shaun often traveled with the team in the fifteen-passenger van. Never without a big sister, someone always escorted him to the boys' restroom.

Around the age of six, Shaun began taking an interest in sports and therefore traveled less. Jarvis missed some of her son's major moments. While away, Shaun hit a home run playing T-Ball for the Blue Jays, breaking a long-standing record. It was in a baseball field where a home run had not been hit in about seventeen years.

"My mother wasn't there to see it because she was traveling with the track team. That really bothered her," he said.

Once retiring from Texas Tech University, Jarvis was able to devote more time to her son's athletic and academic pursuits. Mother, teacher, coach, cheerleader, trainer. She was that and more to Shaun. When he began participating in high school sports, Coach Scott spent a lot of time at Coronado High School in Lubbock, coaching and creating workouts for Shaun.

"I can think of so many times where we would go play catch and do drills," he said. "My mom would sit at our practices and watch me. If she saw something that needed to be improved technically, she would say something to the coaches."

At times Coach Scott would design and implement her own workouts and warm-ups for Shaun. Some of Shaun's teammates thought it was crazy but soon saw the benefits and wanted the benefit of some of Jarvis's knowledge.

Shaun also relished what would become a pregame routine: "It was always a ritual for us to hang out in the living room and just watch TV the night before my baseball games."

As he reflected on his mother's knowledge and skills, Shaun added, "Sometimes, I wish I had stuck with track and field."

Shaun received a full scholarship to and later graduated from West Texas A&M University, in Canyon, Texas, about one hundred miles north of Lubbock. That moment marked one of the proudest for Coach Scott.

Ever wonder how some children view their parents? Shaun saw his mom as kind, a caretaker, great coach, honest, a goal setter, playful, teacher, and a disciplinarian. Olympian never parted his lips, because growing up, there wasn't much mention about the accolades and awards she earned, let alone her Olympic accomplishment.

"But she always found a way to sneak in a message," he said.

There were many lessons Jarvis imparted to Shaun, but none as valuable as the one he carries with him daily: "Don't tell people how good you are, let them tell you how good you are."

One of Jarvis's favorite books is the Bible. The wise words of

Solomon remind me of what she emulated day in and day out. Let someone else praise you, not your own mouth; a stranger, not your own lips. Proverbs 27:2

Coach Scott loved being a mother and was so very proud of her son. "I hit the jackpot. I hope he knows," she said.

After showing me pictures of her granddaughter Skye, she paused and said, "Motherhood is a special gift from above. As we parent, we must not forget to teach."

In my mind's eye, I think about the moments where teaching happened organically. Often, Coach Scott tied the lesson into something that we were experiencing on a personal level. Limitations did not exist as to when or where she taught lessons.

There were also occasions where I thought a harsh consequence would follow. Instead, she would say things like, "Never stop learning." But some admonishments cut deeper than the running consequence.

It was on that day at Buffalo Springs Lake her words pierced. But more than anything, I felt her disappointment.

"Looking back will only cause you to drift ..."

Coach Scott never punished me for looking back, and she did not have to. I never looked back because her reminder, coupled with her disappointment, was enough.

"Remember Lot's wife."

My younger days of Sunday school had kicked in. She did not

have to say much more. In Luke 17:32, Lot's wife looked back to a place that was being destroyed. She also looked back in disobedience. She missed what was ahead by looking back and turned into a pillar of salt.

So ... whatever you are looking back at may not be ruined, but it is behind you for a reason. From that day forward, whether in practice, competition, or a leisure run, I never let up before the finish line.

While some of Coach Scott's methods were described as unconventional or absurd, they worked. Just ask former graduate assistant Jan Chesbro.

"I saw some coaches who would tear kids apart," Jan said. "With Jarvis, it was not like that. She instructed along the way."

Teaching was at the core of everything Coach Scott did. Yet memories of the workouts at the hills, the consequences, nor the lessons ever escaped me.

Years later, we sat watching *Hell's Kitchen* on TV. Celebrity chef Gordon Ramsay had unleashed an arsenal of expletives at another chef about the undercooked meat. As the show cut to commercials, I said, "I thought you were crazy, but not that crazy!"

She grinned. "I wanted you all to learn to discipline your minds like a champion."

A foul word never came out of her mouth. It did not matter. Her beast mode came honest, but so did her strategies for teaching.

After tightening up her headscarf she said, "There were days that I cried. Coach Jones would tell me how great of an athlete I could be. I thought he was just talking to be talking, but the more he said it, the more I believed it. He wanted me to learn to be a competitor."

Jarvis wanted the same for her son and her surrogate children. She transformed practices with all of us to create teachable moments. The great thing is those teaching moments came naturally. The learning spaces could be at practice, in the living room, at a banquet, or in the back seat of a car.

All that I am, I owe to my mother. Jarvis and son, Shaun Scott-Jones

Shaun's wedding day (March 8, 2014)

Leadership Principle #14

Great leaders recognize that fostering learning is not bound by physical space or place. Hence, they constantly look for opportunities to teach life lessons and share their wisdom. They do not restrict themselves to when or where the lesson is taught.

It is easy to find opportunities when you have a connection with those you lead. That is why great leaders are willing to spend quality time with those they lead. It takes work, but it is well worth it.

Great leaders also inspire people to grow. One reason they inspire and empower is because they make the lesson relevant to the individual's situation. Also, because the leader can discern the correct timing of the lesson, wisdom is imparted on those willing to receive it.

But you will not be able to assess your team members' willingness if you do not look for opportunities. Are you ready to teach? Do not miss out. Be intentional and remain committed.

CHAPTER 15

The Call to Overcome Obstacles

> *"We must find the ability to rise if there are no jobs. We must find the ability to rise if there is no food on the table. We must find the ability to rise if there are no clothes on our backs. If I need help, I can ask for something. If you say I can't do something, I will rise. If you hurt or injure me, I will rise. If there are struggles, I will rise. If someone calls me a nasty name, I will rise."—J (January 14, 2010)*

Don't Kick My Door In

Happiness overtook Jarvis as she adored the inside of her new home. The front door opened to the living room, where an oversized window provided light for the pictures that adorned the walls. A bonus room mirrored a time capsule. Dried-out masking tape stuck to the stacked storage bins to identify the enclosed memorabilia.

The 2003–2004 Texas Tech football season kicked off with Mike Leach's fourth year at the helm. Watching the Red Raiders' air raid offense on television came close to topping the move to her new home.

When Jarvis walked into the kitchen, her eyes twitched. "I've had too much Pepsi," she thought.

The stabbing sensation caused her to clench her fists with dread. Before taking a third step, she hit the floor. Jarvis's phone sat on the coffee table. But the weight of maneuvering across the floor caused a disconnect between her brain and body. Like a furious flood, adrenaline rushed through her body. She had no time to panic.

A few minutes passed ... and then hours ... and then darkness faded into days. Four days passed, when the strong odor from her Chihuahua, Cooper, and the buildup of heat overtook the house. Gritty dust and fibers from the brown shaggy carpet plastered her skin. And now Jarvis's body weakened. But sipping on the half bottle of Ozarka' water provided hope. Like a combat soldier, she dug deep and held on to hope.

With hope came help. Home from vacation, Terry, Coach Scott's next-door neighbor, exited his late model pickup and stared at the yard next door. The newspapers sprawled on the lawn. Shaken by a fast-moving train, Terry's premonition overwhelmed him. Walking toward the house, he observed the envelopes and flyers overflowing in the metal mailbox. Terry knocked on the door.

When Coach Scott's faint voice in the distance cried out, adrenaline shot through his body and he prepared himself to knock down the door.

"Don't kick my door in!" Jarvis yelled.

Jarvis tried to drag her body across the floor, but her legs betrayed her. Inch by inch, she summoned strength to her body. Once reaching the door, Jarvis's hand struggled to grip the doorknob. She finally heard the soft click and Terry burst into the house.

Where There's a Wheel, There's a Way

Rehab therapy began four days after Jarvis suffered the debilitating stroke. Paralysis on one side of her body, and pain on the other, made for a lengthy recovery period, but she embraced the battle. After several weeks, Jarvis showed signs of improvement. The fighter stunned the therapists. It didn't take long for them to run out of ideas for her therapeutic workouts. To make sure that every session counted, she began creating and implementing her own rehabilitative workouts.

Released from University Medical Center two-and-a-half months later, the length of the hospitalization paled compared to the first prognosis that Jarvis would never talk, walk, or write again.

Knocked down, but not out. Jarvis refused to surrender to her pain. She prepared for a comeback.

Although Jarvis strode in a manual wheelchair to the Market

Street Grocery Store on 50th Street, she labored to use whatever mobility to make it from her house on 64th Street. Fourteen blocks apart, the distance was nearly two-and-a-half miles each way.

She used her left hand to grip the metal rim and legs to move forward. The cracks and gaps in the pavement made navigation more difficult, but Jarvis did not quit.

She blocked out the pain of the blisters on her palm and the irritating horns of impatient drivers.

The muscle ache and burning shot up her legs. Nausea hit ... she wanted to throw up and wet her parched throat. Determined not to become a prisoner of her pain, she kept pushing. To take her mind off the agony, she gave thanks.

Before long, Jarvis stopped scooting herself down the sidewalk. The noble warrior remained absolute in her resolve to walk. Despite a clenched right hand and an uneven gait, she began pushing her wheelchair to and from the Market Street Grocery Store.

Soon, a walking cane became Jarvis' companion, as she strode to and from the grocery store. "The pain will be there, but you have to work through it. You can always get back what you lost. You may not get all of your tools, but you can still do it," she'd say aloud.

Coach struggled to regain her speech. She tried to overcome her vowels and consonants colliding into one another. To see her mouth turn up and hear her words slur gripped my heart. Just as Jarvis spoke, the words eluded her.

Although she lost full use of her dominant hand, she spent countless hours learning to write with her left hand.

To help with her memory and speech, she watched five televisions in her living room with closed captioning. While listening, she would read the text aloud. Handwritten flashcards to match pictures torn out of the newspaper would also be an aid.

As much as life felt unreal, Jarvis never let down. She relied on the motivational self-talk from *The Little Engine That Could*: "I think I can, I think I can, I think I can!" She would also remind herself, "The sky is not falling."

The positive affirmations made hurting while healing more bearable. "There is no time to give up. There is no time to quit. You always have time to start over and try again," she'd say.

How did she do it?

Several years later, we stood in her backyard at the garden. Three butterflies drank from the mud puddle. Coach Scott moved her water hose.

"It was nature's wisdom that helped me to get through the four days on the floor," she said.

We gazed upon the beauty of the butterflies. For a moment neither of us uttered a word.

And then, as though standing in the Grand Canyon, her words echoed: "I had to adapt and learn to fly. At some point in your life, you will too."

As I ponder that moment in the garden, I reflect on Coach Scott's journey to recovery. I am reminded of the metamorphosis of a butterfly. Rather than striking back, she resolved in her heart that the darkness would not overwhelm her. Instead, she embraced every moment gifted to her and adjusted accordingly. Her admonishment is etched in my mind: "Never give up. No matter how bad you feel, or how bad you think life is toward you."

When difficulties arose, Coach Scott responded with a renewed psyche. She allowed herself to become what no other than the Divine Creator predestined her to be. Just as God programmed every stage of the caterpillar into a butterfly, she knew her steps were ordered.

Visualize a caterpillar for a minute. Imagine if it remained in the chrysalis. Becoming a butterfly is no easy feat. When in the chrysalis, there is no time to rest. And like the caterpillar, you may break to your lowest point. But in that grim hour you can become new if you act. In your dreary place, quitting is not an option. It is your time to rebuild.

Circumstances great or small propelled Coach Scott to keep pushing. And like a butterfly, she set her eyes on a destination. Whatever pain you experience stemming from growth and transformation does not have to last forever.

Coach Scott's comments at the garden also brought back another lesson that I often fall back on. Regardless of what is going on around you, remain faithful and steadfast. Doing so will not only pay off for you but also for those who are a part of your team.

Overcoming obstacles is a key part of leadership. The way you lead your team is pertinent in how your team will respond during difficult times. Depending on how you respond, the team will be able to adapt during adversity and recover at a faster rate.

Leadership Principle #15

Great leaders do not view themselves as a "victim." Think about it. Soldiers do not go into battle expecting to lose the war. There was never a time when Coach Scott thought she would not recover. Instead, she met every obstacle face-to-face and broke down every barrier into small achievable goals.

Great leaders should be like a butterfly and provide resources for others. Coach Scott shared lessons and resources with me and many others. Although you may not see all the seeds you sow come to fruition, be willing to plant the seeds. You may not produce fruit for years to come, but you will yield a harvest at the right time if you don't give up.

Great leaders also see what others cannot. Where others see decline, great leaders see development. Where others see victims, great leaders see victors. And where other leaders see obstacles, great leaders see opportunity.

If willing to seize the opportunity, you too can endure whatever trial you face. That is, if you dig deep, dig wide, and face the obstacle. You can find strength you never knew you had. You can find resilience. You can find hope while in the valley. It is possible if you keep going.

CHAPTER 16

The Call to Know Your Purpose

"Whatever you set out to do in life, know why!"—J

Jarvis's "Why"

Coach Scott fumbled through her red three-ring binder. The stains on the outside were in contrast to the crisp pictures behind the page protectors.

"I wrote my 'why' a long time ago!" she said.

As the last few kernels popped, the warm aroma of popcorn emanated from the kitchen. Glancing at her five TVs, she sat up and squared her shoulders. Her throat cleared before reading aloud.

"To offer responsible coaching and guidance, develop the physical capabilities of athletes maximally, and foster skill, strength, and grace."

She took a sip of her Pepsi and then continued to read the typewritten page. "To contribute to the emotional growth of each athlete." Flipping to the middle of her red binder, she said, "Let me show you something."

It was the *Women Sports* magazine. On the cover, a young queen's hair adorned with black pride and beauty. Cornrows and beads were affixed in Rosalyn Bryant's hair.

In 1975, Coach Scott was competing at Cal State Los Angeles but training with Coach Jones. Bryant was a young sprinter from Chicago. Coach Jones first watched Rosalyn run when she was fifteen years old. While training in Chicago, Rosalyn won many championships, but the one thing eluding her was a spot on the U.S. Olympic team. Training in Chicago would not help her make her dream. The key to accomplishing that goal lay in the capable coaching hands of Fred T. Jones.

Rosalyn made the move to the west coast but had to acclimate to a new turf and teammates.

"What will my teammates be like?" she thought.

Upon meeting Jarvis, the two bonded. "I felt a special connection to Jarvis, and she felt one to me," Rosalyn said.

Like the little sister she never had, Jarvis looked out for Rosalyn in every way.

When Rosalyn arrived at Cal State, there were no dorms and so the girls lived on the upper level of Coach Jones' home. When

Rosalyn found herself challenged by his dictatorship, Jarvis helped her navigate and adjust.

"Don't you worry, I'll take care of Fred," she said.

For Jarvis, it was important to offer support and guidance to Rosalyn. She also believed that independence and privacy were important for the athletes living with Coach Jones. On some occasions, she would reassure Rosalyn and say, "I've known that man a long time. I will handle Fred."

Rosalyn appreciated the support she received from Jarvis but eventually moved out of Coach Jones's home and into the YWCA.

"I just couldn't take it any longer," she said.

Although Rosalyn and Coach Jones parted ways, Rosalyn respected Coach Jones's knowledge on the track and relied on the earlier lessons he taught during workouts.

Like Jarvis, Rosalyn also ran the 400 meters. When she arrived at Cal State, Jarvis had won the 400 meters in the AIAW Championships (1975) and had an American and world record under her belt. She also won the Most Outstanding Athlete Award.

Rosalyn was not the unknown kid for long, as she ran her way into the record books. And yet, no longer garnering the "it" girl status did not deter or disappoint Jarvis. Nor did she become envious of Rosalyn.

Flipping through the magazine, she said, "You've got to take the defeats as well as the victories. Defeats are easier when you have a bond with that person."

Rosalyn qualified for the 1976 Montreal Olympics and won a silver medal in the 4x400 meter relay along with teammates Debra Sapenter, Sheila Ingram, and Pamela Jiles. Rosalyn also competed in the 400 meters, placing fifth in that event.

Before closing her binder, Jarvis said, "My little sister. It was an honor to have Rosalyn as my teammate. She was tough and one of the best competitors to step on the track."

Rosalyn Bryant

Jarvis later parted ways with the L.A. Mercurettes and began training with the Premier Track Club.

The next week Coach Scott and I sat at her favorite restaurant. She pushed aside the basket of cheddar bay biscuits.

"I don't need these," she said. She reached into her pouch. "I brought my papers with me."

Coach Scott wanted to continue with sharing her "why."

"Let's hear it," I said.

"To provide a medium for social and cultural interaction, although not designed or planned." Shifting the papers in her hand, she said, "I always believed I would end up coaching young ladies from diverse backgrounds. I wanted to contribute to better understanding and cooperation among people."

Young ladies from rural, suburban, and urban areas. Low, middle, and high socioeconomic backgrounds. White, Black, Mexican American, Spanish, Asian American. The league of nations. No matter where we came from, we were one.

"Race is only an issue if you allow it to be," she said. She sipped her lemonade and said, "Heck! Man created race anyway."

Coach Scott continued sharing her notes. "Be honest in my coaching, be open-minded, and give my time to help others."

I nodded, and she continued. "Accept constructive criticism, be consistent, and to be an inspiration to my athletes or other coaches."

For example, Beale recognized she and Jarvis would not always agree. As the host of the Southwest Conference Cross Country Meet at Mae Simmons Park, one of Jarvis and Beale's responsibilities included marking the course. Jarvis borrowed the marking machine from the baseball coach.

At the starting line in front of the goal post, Jarvis and Beale stood on the manicured field of grass and readied themselves to make sure the lines were straight. The white powder sputtered out of the machine. As she came around the first curve, Jarvis took a deep breath. She pushed the machine up the hill. When they arrived at the top, the machine quit. One option remained.

"I need you to go to the hardware store to buy fifty cans of aerosol paint," Jarvis said.

"This woman is nuts!" Beale thought. But she drove to the store and returned with ten cans.

"Where are the other forty?"

"I couldn't carry fifty," Beale said.

"Well, spray," Jarvis said.

"I beg your pardon?" Beale said.

"We don't have much time," Jarvis said. "The teams will show up early in the morning, not to mention the sun is about to set."

She started hammering in the flags and left Beale to spray paint the course lines!

Beale sprayed a mile and a half of the course.

The next morning, the aches in her legs registered the 4 a.m. wake-up call. When she arrived at Mae Simmons Park, Beale's pace and grimace told the story.

"You're not sore, are you? We finished the upper part of the hill," Jarvis said.

"We! I'm the one who did all the work!" Beale said.

Jarvis nudged Beale as she chuckled. "It's time you stood up to me."

Beale recalled how her response set their relationship on another trajectory. "It blossomed into something special," she said.

Beale coached at Aledo (Texas) High School for twelve years, followed by Duncanville (Texas) High School for eleven years. Throughout her coaching career, coaches often posed two questions: (1) Where the hell do you get all the quarter-milers? (2) Why do you always have the better jumpers?

Beale's reply was always the same: "Jarvis Scott and Abe Brown. You can read all that you want, but until you transfer it, the students won't get it."

Beale believed that exceptional athletes, such as high jump Olympian Brigetta Barrett, carried the legacy of Jarvis Scott. Why? Because Beale's inspiration to make every one of her athletes run the 400 in training came from Jarvis. Beale learned from Jarvis that running was important for every track athlete. Based on their event, every athlete had to run the 400 meters in a specific time.

"That is from Jarvis Scott," she said.

"I knew the basics and was already a state champion coach, but Jarvis taught me the nuances that allowed me to coach the good to be great, and the great to be exceptional. She had already been to the mountaintop. I was not physically gifted, but she was able to help me combine my technical knowledge with the passion and training methodology that was her trademark. I owe her so much. Every kid I coach has a piece of Jarvis Scott imprinted in their DNA."

As I reflect on the giant of a coach, I cannot help but think that every one of her student-athletes also has a piece of her in their DNA. Coach Scott's impact and influence was limitless because she was intrinsically motivated. She was not worried about awards or her name being in the headlines. Her fulfillment came from watching young adults grow and develop.

Thousands upon thousands of coaches exist in the United States. While they may share the same role, they do it for various reasons. A paycheck, self-promotion, to develop athletic ability, or to develop better people.

All Jarvis wanted to know is if her purpose matched God's plan for her life.

Be it a relationship, career, or another area of our lives, we sometimes wander aimlessly, trying to figure out if we are in the right place. When we are unsure of our position or purpose in life, we end up settling for things that often limit us. But the impact you make on others will go further than you ever imagined. How? If you delight in knowing "why" you do your job, rather than "how" you do your job.

It was easy for Coach Scott to love because she put her purpose before her passion. No matter where we came from, no matter our experiences, and no matter our athletic ability, every story of every student-athlete mattered to her. Be it race, religion, age, gender, or sexual orientation, great leaders lead those who are different from them.

Jarvis and Beale at Mae Simmons Park

Leadership Principle #16

Great leaders know their purpose. There is no microwave solution to help you figure out your purpose in life. The one constant is you. Begin with understanding who you are. The real you. Dig deep. Work toward your purpose. Your "what" in your personal or professional career is not enough. Some lead for an outcome while others lead regardless of the outcome. No one wants a losing team, but great leaders recognize that the outcome is beyond the score-board. Why? Because great leaders understand they can always improve, and therefore others around them can always improve.

Good leaders look for people who can produce results while great leaders look for people who can build on relationships. Those people will do whatever it takes because they trust you, because they care about you, because they are vested in the outcome as much as you. More importantly, they know their leader cares about them.

Because Coach Scott understood her "why," neither her labor nor legacy would be in vain. What about you?

CHAPTER 17

The Call to Appreciate Feedback

> *"If you never see their face again ...*
> *if you never hear their voice again ... hold on to*
> *the memories, because they are precious."—J*

To J with Love

Once retired, Coach Scott led a quiet and private life. Many of her friends and former teammates lost contact. Although distance and time may have separated them, she would cherish the pictures, notes, letters, and cards until her passing. Every moment she spent with family, friends, and student-athletes mattered.

In a faded red binder with black netting, she kept pictures of many close friends, former athletes, and former teammates. One was Mrs. Bea Rainey Johnson, who organized and found Premier Track Club in August 1973. There had been no organized program for girls in the East Los Angeles–Alhambra area.

"I never understood what made her leave Fred Jones and come to Premier, but I was glad she did," Bea said.

While the two would lose touch, Jarvis held on to pictures and a postcard from Bea:

December 1975 (Bea)
Hey Jaye! Have been missing you but having a nice time. Not doing much here, but being very lazy. I will be home on the 1st, will arrive at 7:15. Will be glad to see you. Love, Bea

Thank you for being a friend and coach. Bea Rainey-Johnson

And whether student-athletes reached higher heights athletically, it did not matter to Coach Scott. She endeavored to impact. Jarvis ended her tenure at Cal State Los Angeles as an assistant coach to become the first African American head coach at Texas Tech University. For those who knew Jarvis, it was evident that Texas Tech had chosen a winner. Jeannine McHaney, Women's Administrator for Texas Tech Athletics was relentless in her pursuit of Jarvis. An advocate for women's sports, she didn't allow Jarvis' first "no" to stop her from going after the thirty-two-year-old. When Jarvis did accept the offer, her buddy Martha was especially proud as the below note demonstrates. The following note speak for themselves.

September 10, 1979

Dear Jeanine,

Just a note of appreciation to you. The growth of women's sports programs in the country has moved very slowly during the seventeen years of my athletic career. The growth I refer to is of qualified and dedicated administrators (coaching falls in this category). There have always been good people ... just not enough. A big part of this problem is the fact that many athletes after their competitive careers decide not to stay involved. Jarvis is an exception to the rule. She has given enough of herself to fill the shoes of ten. You have a JEWEL. I especially want to say thank you for two reasons: Jarvis is a good friend of mine and so is track and field. The fact that you wanted a black person on your staff but did not give up quality in the process.

Sincerely,

Martha Watson (1968 Olympic Long Jumper)

March 19, 1981

4-time Olympian,
Martha Watson

Jeannine McHaney;
Pioneer and Women's
Athletic Director,
Texas Tech University

Coach Jones was also proud and wanted Jarvis' colleagues to know. Below is a letter he wrote Gerald Meyers, the head men's basketball coach.

Dear Gerald,

You have as a coworker one of the finest athletes in Jarvis Scott. I also can't say enough about Jarvis as a person. As you've found out, she's of the highest integrity and full of warmth and kindness. I wouldn't hesitate in the least sending any of my top female or male athletes to your program. As things develop, I'll let you know.

Regards,

Fred Jones (Head Men and Women's Coach) West Los Angeles College

Coach Scott not only aspired to be the best but wanted the same for her student-athletes. She did as her father admonished— she left her ego behind and allowed her actions to speak for themselves. Selfless as much as successful, Coach Scott was purposeful about impacting the lives of others.

One of her athletes was Michele Hopper. She was seventeen years old when she met Jarvis.

"She was such a mentor to me coming out of high school. I didn't know how far I could run after high school until I met Jarvis," Michele said.

Aside from competing for Cal State Los Angeles, Michele also ran for the West Team when Jarvis coached for the South Team at the United States Olympic Festival. Jarvis attributed the start of Premier Track Club's success to Michele. Below is a note and poem written to Jarvis from Michele.

Jarvis,

Good luck in New York! Even though I'm in LA physically, mentally I'll be with you all the way in New York. I sure wish I could come see you run 'cause I know it's gonna be something to see. All week I've been having good feelings about this weekend. You look super and I know you're ready! Got the best coach and I know she'll look after you. Have a good time and I'll miss ya partner! Good luck, Hop

The poor girl struggled to win the race.

She collapsed when the others picked up the pace.

One by one they passed her so fast.

It broke her heart to think she'd be last.

What killed her was that refusal to lose.

She now rests in peace in her track shoes.

The last home stretch hurt quite a bit.

As a result, she now lies in the long jump pit.

For years she fought to be number one

Her dying words were Why did I run?

Michele Hopper

Jarvis also formed a strong bond with Michele's parents, as shown in the following note.

February 1976

Dear Jarvis,

The Senior Citizens at "428" wish to the very best in New York. Have a good trip and a good race. We will be thinking about you! Best wishes always. Michele Hopper's mom and Dad (Marshall and Ruth Hopper)

It's not often that your childhood hero remains your hero into adulthood, but that's what happened for Carol Dawson as she embarked on a career in track and field.

Michele Hopper

Jarvis coached Carol, a young white girl, at the 1977 Junior Olympics.

"She was an amazing human being," Carol said of Jarvis. "She was just a phenomenal person."

Skin color was never an issue, as they shared a strong bond.

Carol's voice softened as she said, "There was no race when we were together. She loved me and I loved her the same. All I knew is there was this fantastic woman who believed in me and loved me."

Carol credited Jarvis as the reason she went on to run track in high school. The opportunities and famous athletes she met will always be a precious memory. One of her favorite memories was meeting Jesse Owens and getting his autograph on her medal. An expression of appreciation is in the following letter written by Carol's mom to the organizer of the Junior Olympics:

August 19, 1977

Dear Mr. Cuzic,

I wish to express my thanks to you and the City of Los Angeles for the marvelous experience my daughter, Carol Dawson, has just enjoyed at the ARCO Jesse Owens Games. She especially loved working with her coach, Jarvis Scott. Jarvis is a very warm, supportive person; she helped Carol through many anxious moments. The bronze medal she will cherish and keep safely, but the feelings she has inside and the encouragement and support she was given by Jarvis she will never forget. Jarvis is just a great person and a good example for impressionable children. All the work in planning and organizing this event was evident by the smooth and professional manner in which the meet was conducted. You and your staff are to be commended for this and I was proud to be a participant from the host city. Again, my thanks to you for allowing Carol the opportunity in her early years to have learned so much.

Sincerely,

Lanie Dawson

Often, students, athletes, or participants in extracurricular activities don't always recognize their full potential, let alone put in the work to unlock it.

When others recognize your gift, you should act upon the contributions they have made to your continuing growth and success.

Your position or title may change, but you can still find ways to bring out the best in others. When you take the time to mentor, your return on investment is much higher than when no deposits are made. As you begin to climb the ladder of success, don't forget the rungs can be used for others to reach higher heights.

Even as she made the professional transition to an assistant coach and head coach, Jarvis still offered her time, expertise, and talent to others. The following letters are from Laura LaRosa, an 8th grade student who ran in the Jim Bush Camp, located in San Diego, California.

August 18, 1978

Dear Jarvis,

Received your letter OK! I understood it well. The Jim Bush track camp really taught me many things I didn't know. And I hope next year I can go again. The stuff you wrote in the letter I understand well. The exercises were well-explained by different coaches of the camp so that helps me a lot. If the coaches didn't tell me how to do them, I never would have known how! When I was at the camp, there was a misunderstanding! If you remember, we had to go to our stretching groups and that was at about nine to ten every morning. And after I had worked with the 880 group I didn't realize that I wasn't in the 440-220-100 stretching group. For about the third day, but I didn't ever tell, I was in the wrong group, so my question is, could I just do the exercises that Coach Larson and Coach Kota explained to us? They are the distance runners and they were talking to us about the stretching for 880 and up, but I needed 440 and down, so could I just do the stretching exercises that they told me or what? But as far as the exercises in your letter, I understand them well and I will start working out by your workout list as soon as August 21 comes around, but until that I will jog. Thanks again and call me when you receive this if you question the letter.

Love, Laura LaRosa

September 1978

Jarvis,

I'm really sorry about not writing sooner, but I've been really busy with school homework and your workouts you send me. They are all fun. Some of my friends go with me and they do what I have to do. One day I was on the track and doing 110s working on form and it was on the curve. This lady comes on the track and starts stretching and then she started to run and then I started doing 110s on the straight and she comes up to me and asked what grade I was in. I said 8th and she said, "OH, you don't go to Terra Nova (a high school)?" I said no I go to Ortega, and she asked my name. I said Laura LaRosa and she asked me if I was interested in cross country or track and field and I said yes I am. And she said I have to tell Coach Figler about you. He's a track coach at Terra Nova. I was happy. School started for us and my PE coach has us already jogging and stretching. He makes us do a mile a day and stretch before and after. His name is Mr. Berrin. I told Mrs. Karl and Mr. Berrin about you and your running career and they really thought it was great and so do I. So thanks again for the training workouts. I will follow them 100 percent.

Love, Laura LaRosa

P.S. The workouts are making me better.

March 8, 1979

Dear Jarvis,

Hi how have you been? I hope well. Looking forward to 1980? Or are you participating in the Olympics? I am going to watch them on TV for sure. So how have you been otherwise? I got a few papers on the "Jim Bush Camp." Saw your picture and the little article to go with it. It was a good picture. Looks just like you!! (of course) So I guess you're planning on being a coach for his great camp. I asked my mom about going and she said, well, that's a long time away so we will see. I am trying to talk my friends in to going. I got some to go and some don't know. The real reason I wrote was to let you know I will be participating in Pacifica's (my city) Jr. Olympics for 7th and 8th grade girls and boys. In Pacifica and you can win a trophy. For the most outstanding runner of Pacifica, plus ribbons you could win. Last year I ran in it and won 5 first place ribbons and the trophy for the 7th grade. However, that was when I was in shape! And right now I'm not in that good of shape. And I want to win the trophy again this year, but at the rate I am going, I really don't know! So my question is, should I just do the workouts that you assigned to me in the summer or just plan on jogging? I still do jogging up in the mountains and it was hard but it all will be paid back by that trophy. The next day after the hill work, I tried to go out and jog three to four miles and I felt really tired like my body wouldn't let me go, and I wanted to, but on account of that I did about two-and-a-half to three miles. My question is, how many miles should I do after doing a hard eight- to nine-mile course of mountains? Our Jr. Olympics will be in the middle of May, which is about two months, so I need to get in shape for it. So do you think I can get in shape in two months to win the trophy? What kind of work should I do to get ready? The events I will be running are the 440, 220, 440-yard relay, 880. I will be throwing the softball, and maybe running the long jump. I hope you will be able to help me to figure a workout plan to help me win! Well, I better go. Thank you again.

Love, Laura LaRosa Write back soon please.

P.S. I bought a book on running and I was looking in it and you were in it with a white woman and you sorta had your arms around her. "Great, Jarvis."

Jarvis did not have a team full of All-Americans, but that didn't matter. Her main goal was to equip young women and men with life skills that would help propel us in our respective careers. Whatever the need, she was always happy to assist.

A woman of many firsts, it was no surprise that Sharon Moultrie would embody similar characteristics of Coach Scott and amass accolades. The long jumper hailing from Pampa, Texas, in the northern part of the state, became Texas Tech University's first All-American in any sport. She would also become the university's first black homecoming queen. Below is a letter Sharon wrote Coach Scott three days before graduation.

May 10, 1983

Dear Jarvis,

It's really hard for me to put this down on paper, but the time has come. I've put this off for about a week now. If there is a reason for me to say I don't want to leave Lubbock, that reason would be you. Well, where do I begin? I can't thank you enough for the influence and the big part you've played in my life these years at Tech. You have been so much more than a coach. I honestly think of you as a mother away from home, a sister, a counselor, and lastly a great friend. I could go on forever with this (smile). I certainly wish all other athletes you have coached would've and can have the great relationship we have. I know this isn't possible, but look at it this way. It's their loss (smile). When I look at your philosophy, your goals, and your aspects you have on life, I realized that these things were accomplished through hard work and dedication. I know good things and deserving things are earned. I really would like to say that I'm following in your footsteps, but I still have many giant steps to make, and I'm no quitter (smile). Everything hasn't been peachy, but we stuck to it. ... Black people go through hard times, they have family problems, but they struggle to survive. God's guidance, support from my family, you, and friends have given me determination to be somebody. Jarvis, I'm really gonna miss you. I sat here teary-eyed because I can't believe I'm actually writing this. Overall, this has been four great years. Thanks again for your love, support, guidance, friendship, determination, and motivation. You are a super person. May God bless you. You'll never be forgotten.

Sharon Moutrie '83

Sharon Moultrie the day before the AIAW Outdoor Championships

Motivated to mentor; Falecia Freeman, Jarvis Scott, and Sharon Moultrie.

Sheryl Estes competed in track and field for Texas Tech during the 1980-1981 school year. A middle and long distance runner, she set a school record in the 1000 yards (1981). Sheryl transferred to West Texas State (now A&M), where she played basketball (1981-1984).

Jarvis,

I just wanted to write and thank you for the job recommendation. With your help, I got a job at Canyon High School. I'll be the Assistant Basketball and Track Coach for girls and the Head Cross Country Coach for boys and girls. I'm really looking forward to it and I think it'll be a good job to start out with. I could really use your help on the cross country part of it. If you have time, I'd appreciate some information. If you could send me an outline of your progression of the training season and some sample workouts of each type of training, it would help me get started. Just send me any information that would help me. Once again, I'd like to thank you for all your help.

Sincerely,

Sheryl Estes

February 1985

Sheryl Estes

When Jerri Howell transferred from East Texas State (Commerce) to Texas Tech University, she decided to try out for the women's track team. To Jerri's surprise, she not only made the team, but later earned a partial scholarship. Tabbed a utility runner, Jerri ran everything from the sprint relay, 400 meters, 800 meters and cross country.

Jerri heeded Coach Scott's advice to meet people where they are. More than anything, she loved that Coach Scott walked the walk. "She never called me out, but instead, she would pull us aside to talk to and plant seeds." The following is a note Jerri wrote in a card she sent Coach Scott shortly after graduating.

Coach Scott and Jerri Howell at the Texas Tech Invitational

I got this card because it symbolizes all that you have done for me. You served as sort of my crutch for the last few years; you never let me fall. I know that that crutch will always be with me with all of the knowledge you have taught me. I have learned so much from you and have succeeded because of you. Thanks for all your help and support. Good luck this season and for the future.

Love you,

Jerri Howell

Nancy King tried out for the track team in the spring of 1984 and earned a scholarship the following year. She competed in the 5,000 meters and 10,000 meters. Unfortunately her athletic career was cut short due to an Achilles injury. Nancy struggled with her hopes at an Olympic bid ending. But the encouragement from

Coach Scott helped her through some of her most difficult days. Below is a letter Nancy wrote Coach Scott.

August 27, 1986

Dear Jarvis,

I hope everything is going well for you. I thought I would drop you a letter to thank you for our talk back in July. I don't think you will ever realize how much inspiration you have given me the past few years. Things are going real well for me now. I'm working and going to school at a Community College here in Dallas. I've also been keeping up with my writing career. I wanted you to read one of my latest works. I've enclosed it with this letter. The reason I wrote it was because you were always telling me I had to do some soul-searching. Well, I think I'm finally starting to get the hang of it. I hope you keep it and read it whenever things are rough and you feel a little lost. Who knows, someone else on the team may need a little soul-searching. You're welcome to share this with anyone who might need it. Anyway, good luck this fall and hopefully I'll be transferring back to Tech in the Spring.

Thank You,

Nancy

Givings of the Heart by Nancy King

Here I am, living beside myself, always looking in from the outside.

Searching myself for the true meaning of existence.

Trying to find out exactly what I had to
give and what I had left to keep.

I've suffered for so long, dreading on all that I've done wrong.

I'm not the only one who has felt the shame
or the burning flame of disgrace.

I guess it's just a part of this crazy human race.

I know I've changed through the years and
have surrendered a great many tears.

But I do believe that it's all for the better.

Now I'm much stronger and able to stand on my own.

To understand yourself is to be only your true self.

I realize now that I need to strive to be the best that I can be.

It's the only way to make it through each day.

I set my soul free, I've found out the hidden sky.

The givings of the heart is the only place that I can start.

With this I now can show the meaning of my
true self, with the givings of my heart.

Nancy King

Interesting to think how a card or letter can create such appreciation.

Take a cue from J ... take time to appreciate feedback.

In doing so, our needs become secondary.

The privilege of Jarvis's career was not the 1968 Olympics. It was not being the first African American head coach at Texas Tech University. It was not being the first and only American female athlete to double in the 400 meters and 800 meters in the Olympics. It was not being the first American athlete to make the finals in the 400 meters in the Olympics. Nor being selected to the Los Angeles CIS Hall of Fame or Cal State Los Angeles Hall of Fame. Nor the sixth-place finish at the Olympics.

The privilege was all hers to assemble a group of young men and women who would become coaches, teachers, counselors, doctors, nurses, artists, editors, and authors.

"I get joy in watching you all accomplish your goals," she said. "My time is up."

Leadership Principle #17

Leaders who appreciate feedback are not worried about who said what, but more so about what is being said. Embracing the feedback demonstrates an ability to grow. More importantly, it demonstrates an acknowledgment that feedback is about a dialogue, rather than a monologue.

CHAPTER 18

The Call to Let Go

"I will win."—J

Prepared for Paradise

A little over thirty-one years after stepping foot on the campus of Texas Tech University, on August 4, 2017, Coach Scott, sitting in her living room, said, "I'm going to write a book."

On her coffee table sat a red, three-ring, one-inch poly binder. The Schoolio Von Hoolio sticker from Office Max was still affixed to the front. Never one to let anything go to waste, she would use loose construction paper, one-sided mail advertisements, and anything with at least one blank side to journal her thoughts and the significant events in her life.

Sadly, she never got the opportunity.

On September 29, 2017, Coach Scott laid down to nap. But

while lying on her living room couch, she entered eternal rest. My body collapsed upon hearing the news. Sitting on the dining room floor, my tears clouded the numbers on my keypad. But hearing my mom's voice on the other end must have been comforting and cathartic all at the same time.

"Coach Scott is gone," I said, whimpering.

"Oh baby," she said.

Sorrow quickly consumed the emptiness as I tried to gasp for air. Although I knew it would not be the last time, I cried; it was my mom's words that soothed my pain.

"It's OK. She ran an amazing race."

As I began wiping the tears from my face, I thought about the perseverance and patience that Coach Scott possessed. All that she demonstrated mirrored a race of faith. With fervency and focus, she allowed nothing to hinder her progress. I can't help but think that of all her races, the race of life was the most important. The spiritual race.

The following week I sat in the parking lot and gathered myself. A sense of pride and doom engulfed me. I walked in and handed Coach Scott's Olympic uniform and pictures to Willie Griffin, Jr., the funeral director.

"Please guard these with your life," I said.

"We will take excellent care of them. Loved ones bring precious items all the time," he said.

A few moments later I sat in the office. The staff person handed me the funeral program. I smiled, but the tears still soaked my cheeks.

And for the briefest of moments, I was reminded of my mom's words: "She ran an amazing race."

The Apostle Paul asked a question in 1 Corinthians 9:24. "Do you not know that in a race, all the runners run, but only one receives the prize? So run that you may obtain it."

Gratitude filled my heart that Coach Scott chose to stay in the race. Why? Because she valued the prize.

Walking out of the funeral home, I noticed a butterfly perched on the sidewalk with its wings folded. Undisturbed, the traffic noises did not seem to bother the butterfly.

As I walked to my car, the butterfly reappeared, and overwhelming joy consumed me. I extended my arm, but the palm of my hand never became a landing spot. And as it took flight, I smiled and said, "Jarvis is for butterfly."

When I arrived home, I could not help but think about the butterfly. I began to read about monarch butterflies. Fascinated about their journey to Mexico, I believed the butterfly was a sign.

On October 7, 2017, there was no huge fanfare. In an intimate setting, many former student-athletes, community, and one former coworker sat in New Hope Missionary Baptist Church to memorialize the monarch. With no church affiliation that I knew of, Pastor Larry S. Polk graciously opened the doors of the church for the service at no cost. Lubbock Community Ushers served in a capacity as though Coach Scott was a fellow doorkeeper. We were favored with two songs beautifully sung by Latrice Godfrey: *I Can Only Imagine* and *When you Hear of My Homegoing*. We laughed and cried hearing the stories from former student-athletes as well as Olympic teammates Barbara Ferrell-Edmonson and Tom Lough. The eulogist, Pastor DeShun Avery, preached a sermon titled "Run with Purpose."

Eight days after the memorial service, I received an email stating that Coach Jones wanted me to please call at the number listed. I could detect the age in his voice. Feeble and yet somber, he wanted confirmation that the woman he coached to stardom had passed away. Coach Jones thought Jarvis died in 2003, because of complications from her stroke. This time, the obituary someone had placed in his mailbox made it a sad reality. The pride in his voice as he spoke about Jarvis was so clear.

"She never gave me any problems," he said. "I coached a lot of Olympians and world-class athletes but none as tough as her. No one worked as hard as Jarvis."

It had been forty-nine years and three days since the opening ceremonies of the 19th Olympiad in Mexico City. For Coach Fred T. Jones, it seemed like yesterday. He continued to gloat about his "girl," and then paused. I could hear the faint sound of *Family Feud* in the background, before he said, "I will never understand why."

Nearly fifty years later, the eighty-three-year-old, long retired, grieved two deaths. First, Jarvis relinquishing her Olympic spot in the 800 meters, and second, her physical death. Yet he found some consolation that Jarvis's story would be shared with many.

"I am going to send you some pictures," he said.

Fred Jones was no longer the spry Gunnery Sergeant. It was hard for me to hear or pick up clues of a controlling or mean man. Close to fifty years later, the calloused person juxtaposed to the softness of his voice, which now sounded like Mr. Rogers.

Coach Jones followed up the phone call with a text message: "Thanks again for making contact with me. I felt so close with Jarvis by talking with u. I went over my notes forty-nine years ago (memory is not as precise as it used to be). I was there in Mexico at the time of the 400 meters and not after, as I once thought. Because I now remember arranging the financing for the transportation and entertainment while in Mexico (like going to the nightclub there) for Barb Ferrell's and Jarvis's mom. All-expenses paid, including tickets to the competition, so they can watch their daughters compete on the world stage. Both families were very poor, especially Jarvis's. I think this was Jarvis's driving force. She was intent on improving her lot in life."

Not only was she intent on improving her life but the life of others. The story of the butterfly needs to continue. Jarvis Scott's life, labor, and leadership represented a butterfly. Change and transformation. Why? Because her start in life differed from the end. Like a butterfly, she crawled before she walked and did not resist the struggle while in the cocoon. Coach Scott flew high.

Like a butterfly, while Coach Scott may have taken her last flight, she left instructions on how to increase the population of leaders. Think about it. Butterflies move from bush to bush. It is not for their own benefit but for the benefit of others.

As a child, I remember hearing meteorologists on television say that butterflies could flap their wings in Brazil and then cause a tornado in Texas. Yes ... the Butterfly Effect is real! Perhaps not when it comes to weather patterns but certainly when it comes to our interactions with others.

The smallest changes in the way we talk and treat one another can have a large impact and influence on the lives of others. Your role as a leader is not limited to a position or title. Nor is it limited to a certain number of days, months, or years. What you seed into the lives of others can ultimately be like the Butterfly Effect and have an immeasurable impact.

No one had to sell Coach Scott on the necessity of leadership. Whether we knew it or not, or for that matter, liked it or not, Coach Scott's determination to equip us with the skills and tools necessary to navigate through life never waned. Her willingness to share her gift helped to unwrap potential in all her prodigies. Like a butterfly, her peripheral vision was so good, it allowed her to see the wings of others. She intentionally pollinated and produced offspring, to help others soar. And perhaps behind her mirrored shades she possessed ultraviolet vision so she could see past what others could not, or just were not trying to see.

Not always an easy task, there was no convincing her that leadership did not matter! And leadership should matter to you too.

You have an amazing opportunity ahead of you. The leadership style you develop can either work for you or against you. The decision is yours. You can unleash attributes that will inspire and impact others for a lifetime.

A metamorphic approach to leadership can begin today. Like a butterfly, effective leadership does not occur over night. But you can commit to going through the process.

Once again, here are the leadership principles modeled by Coach Jarvis Scott:

1. You must first change your mind-set.
2. Learn to respond and not react. Manage your emotions to prevent frustration, fatigue, and failure.
3. Do not yield to resistance. Know when to push and when to pull.
4. Keep good company. Make sure you have the right people in your circle.

5. Along the way some people will hurt you. Be it emotional or physical pain, learn to forgive.

6. Set goals to give yourself a sense of direction and a target to reach.

7. Difficulties will arise but remember to become a part of the solution.

8. Practice selfless humility, by putting the needs of others in front of your personal desires.

9. To get the best out of your team, stay focused.

10. Because you cannot do everything on your own, know when and how to delegate.

11. Creating a culture of fairness helps everyone stay accountable for the choices they make.

12. Learn from the past, by learning from the wisdom of previous generations.

13. Empathize with your team.

14. Create teachable moments.

15. You will have setbacks, but do not give up. Dig deep so that you can overcome obstacles.

16. If you want to live a meaningful life, know your purpose.

17. Appreciate feedback.

And when it is time to let go, your work will speak for you. Imagine all the lovely things that can emerge because of your leadership. And to think that beauty can come from a caterpillar. Yes, a caterpillar.

Transformation is a process and a rebirth. It is about your willingness to do what Steve Harvey says, and "jump." It is about listening to that still and quiet voice of God and be what He called you to be. To be the leader He called you to be, you must do what He called you to do. Are you ready to jump? It's time to fly!

ODE TO JARVIS SCOTT
by Jarvis Scott

Jarvis is a woman with a lot of soul, Jarvis is a
wonderful person with a heart of gold.

Jarvis is a woman, shaped from a perfect mold.
But oh! Jarvis Scott, is cold, cold, cold!

She's generous, kind and often bold. She
keeps my heart with a strong hold.

Jarvis will be wonderful even when she grows
old, but oh! Jarvis Scott, she is so cold!

I love her more and more each day. Sometimes
I don't even know what to say.

There's a lot of love in my heart untold,
but Jarvis Scott, Oh she's so cold!

One of these days, she won't be cold! Out from her heart
will pour all of her soul, that's buried beneath the ice and
snow, and she will be out of sight, in my heart I know.

Acknowledgments

No journey is meant to be a solo trip. I am filled with gratitude when I reflect upon my support system who helped make this book a reality. I am most grateful to my Lord and Savior for provision and guidance throughout this process. Without him, none of this would be possible.

As I reflect on my first playmates, my heart smiles. Of all the many lessons and laughs, an essential truth stands out. That is, if I have my brothers and sisters, I will always have a cheering section. Janet, Diane, Rob, and Dwayne. Thank you! Even when the fight was fixed, you stayed in my corner.

To my nieces, nephews, great nieces, and great nephews (you know who you are): My hearts desire is that you blaze the path God has set for you, love like there is no tomorrow, find strength during struggles, and keep the faith even when the finish line appears far.

Interwoven in athletics is the gift of relationships. The instrumental role of the 1968 Olympic teammates of Jarvis Scott who provided interviews cannot be overlooked. A special thanks to Mrs. Barbara Ferrell-Edmonson, Mrs. Madeline Manning-Mimms, Mrs. Martha Watson, Mrs. Doris-Brown Heritage, and Mr. Reynaldo Brown. Not once did any of you hesitate to assist me along this journey. And yet there were teammates such as Mrs. Wyomia Tyus and Dr. John Carlos who I did not interview, but their encouraging words helped me to believe I could soar. Simply because I was connected to Jarvis "Jaye" Scott, the support was solidified, and never ending.

I realize I am the recipient of the gift Jarvis desired for every student-athlete... Teamwork. Thank you to my Texas Tech teammates and former assistant coaches of Jarvis Scott for the stories told and untold. Your support and excitement throughout this journey have kept me going. To Sharon Moultrie-Bruner, Maria Medina-Barros, Ronnie Green, Leonard Harrison, Jeffrey "Red Cloud" Barros, Georgianna Jones-Hallman, Yvette Patterson (deceased), Beale Tolbert, Jan Chesbro-Wohlschlag, Nancy King, Amie Frescaz-Kraenzel, Sheryl Estes, and Jerry Howell-Webb: Thank you for helping to ensure that Jarvis' legacy continue, and her labor not be in vain. Special thanks to Texas Tech Athletics Communications for the open door to obtain whatever photos, as well as permission to use photos.

I am indebted to Jarvis' Cal State and Premier Track Club family: Rosalyn Bryant-Clark, Michele Hopper-Buchicchio, and

Mrs. Beatrice Raney-Johnson. No matter the time of the day, you answered questions, looked at pictures, encouraged me, and helped me to fill in the gaps. Thank you! Also, I am grateful to Cal State LA Athletics for permission to use photos.

As adolescents, some people become sponges and soak in the wisdom to later share with others. Laura LaRosa is one example. I am grateful that your short time spent with Jarvis enabled you to impact others in the social work profession.

I would like to express my deepest gratitude to Joyce James, William Doctor, Jr., Norbert Elliott, Rose Mary Wiley, and Janna Aycock. Your generosity and support helped to make this book a reality. I will never forget your kindness.

Everyone needs an Ardie Mae Langston in their life. Thank you, Ardie for being a listening ear, cheerleader, encourager, and my ride or die. More importantly, I am grateful for your gift of friendship. Because no matter the tide, you rode every wave with me.

My only wish is that Jarvis could have met one of the most intelligent, empathetic, and empowering educators as well as Biblical and Social Justice Advocate's known to man. George Lee Love, Jr., your reminders, and nudges have not gone unnoticed. Words are not enough to convey my gratitude. Because you saw the value in Coach Scott's story, you provided inspiration and constant reminders to run towards the roar.

I would like to express my deepest appreciation to professionals who do it best in their respective fields. Sarah Brown, thank you for pushing me through inquiry, reflection, and your invaluable insight. During difficult moments, you provided guidance with one simple question: "What would Jarvis do?" And to Cristina Smith and Debra Englander, I appreciate your willingness to jump in and help whenever needed. Additionally, Rachel Schuster, your dearth of knowledge, expertise, and kindness is just what a first-time author like me needed. Thank you does not seem to be enough! To Jerry Dorris, thank you for your patience. I gave a lot of no's but you hung in there with me. More importantly, your willingness to tend to every detail of the cover and interior design produced the results I hoped for.

To my photographer, Pamela Tuckey. Thank you for using your gift to help me share Coach Scott's story.

To my pastor, DeShun Avery. What can I say? You have mastered the art of servant leadership that Jarvis longed for others to possess. Your heart for people truly embodies a beacon of light and restores faith in humanity.

To Larry S. Polk, pastor of New Hope Missionary Baptist Church (Lubbock). Thank you for opening the doors of your church to honor the life of Coach Jarvis Scott. I will never forget your words, "We got you." And from that day forward, you have kept your word. I appreciate you.

Often, coaches don't get the credit that is due to them. Beginning in Junior High, I was blessed with track and field coaches, who impacted and inspired me and many other student-athletes. To Lisa Phelps, Lucy Neiman, Abe Brown (deceased), and Norbert Elliott. Thank you for looking beyond the win-loss column. Thank you for caring. More importantly, thank you for never abandoning your calling to shape the lives of student-athletes.

Lastly, thank you to my test readers (William Boynton, William Doctor, Jr., Dina Jeffries, and George Lee Love, Jr.) for taking out time of your busy schedules to read my manuscript. Not only did you read the manuscript, but you answered questions and provided feedback. Because of your time and efforts, I am confident that I've written a book that would make Coach Scott proud.

About the Author

Dr. Amanda Banks has served in leadership roles in education, churches, nonprofits, and civic groups in Lubbock, Texas. A former All-American in the Triple Jump, she is a member of the Texas Tech Hall of Fame and Southwest Conference Hall of Fame.

The executive director of the May Youth Foundation, Dr. Banks earned her Ph.D. from Texas Tech University in Counselor Education. Also a race and gender equity consultant, she is devoted to exploring the hidden treasures of women and other marginalized populations. Additionally, Dr. Banks is a writer for the TV show *Their Life, My Lens* and the award winning *A Fishing Story*.

A recipient of the Woman of the Year/Outstanding Mentor Award by Delta Sigma Theta Sorority, Inc. Lubbock Alumnae

Chapter, Dr. Banks is also a church drill team and praise dance instructor. When she is not writing or working in her community, Dr. Banks enjoys running, playing tennis, and collecting sports cards.

To contact Dr. Banks and find out about training and speaking engagements, visit request www. GetAmazingRace.com.

ENDNOTES

1   "Fannie Lou Hamer" PBS. Public Broadcasting Service. Accessed February 10, 2019. https://www.pbs.org/wgbh/americanexperience/features/freedomsummer-hamer.

2   "Fannie Lou Hamer" PBS. Public Broadcasting Service. Accessed February 10, 2019. https://www.pbs.org/wgbh/americanexperience/features/freedomsummer-hamer.

3,4 The Watts Riots, 50 Years Later. Accessed August 28, 2018. https://www.cbsnews.com/news/watts-riots-50-years-later/

5   History.com Editors. "Watts Rebellion." History.com. A&E Television Networks, September 28, 2017. https://www.history.com/topics/1960s/watts-riots.

6   Rustin, Bayard. "The Watts 'Manifesto' and the McCone Report by Bayard Rustin." Longform, March 1, 1966. https://longform.org/posts/the-watts-manifesto-the-mccone-report.

7   Reft, Ryan on September 2. "Structured Unrest: The Rumford Act, Proposition 14, and the Systematic Inequality that Created the Watts Riots." Tropics of Meta, April 28, 2015. https://tropicsof meta.com/2014/09/02/structured-unrest-the-rumford-act-proposition-14-and-the-systematic-inequality-that-created-the-watts-riots/.

8   Ladenburg, Thomas. "African Americans in the Land of Equality." 1974, 1998, 2001, 2007. https://www.digitalhistory.uh.edu

9   "Events." Civil Rights Digital Library. Accessed June 11, 2018. https://crdl.usg.edu/events/.

10 "Fist of Freedom: An Olympic Story Not Taught in School." Accessed November 3,

2018. https://www.pbs.org/newshour/extra/app/uploads/2014/02/All-docs-for-Human-Rights-lesson-2.pdf.

11 "Fist of Freedom: An Olympic Story Not Taught in School." Accessed November 3, 2018. https://www.pbs.org/newshour/extra/app/uploads/2014/02/All-docs-for-Human-Rights-lesson-2.pdf.

12 "Mexico's 1968 Massacre: What Really Happened?" NPR. NPR, December 1, 2008. https://npr.org/templates/story/story.php?storyId=97546687

13 USA Track and Field and Hymans, R. (2008) "The History of the United States Olympic Trials: Track and Field." https://www.usatf.org

14 Amistad Research Center. "African American Athletes." Amistad Research Center, July 27, 2012. https://amistadresearch.wordpress.com/category/african-american-athletes/.

PHOTO CREDITS

Chapter 1

♦ Jarvis Lavonne Scott; Easter Sunday; Precious Memories and Stability in the Arms: Courtesy of the Estate of Jarvis Lavonne Scott

Chapter 2

♦ Watts Riots photos: Los Angeles Sentinel Newspaper, Courtesy of Los Angeles County Library, Black Resource Center
♦ Jarvis Scott Pan Am Games Team Photo: Courtesy of U.S. Olympic & Paralympic Committee Archives

Chapter 3

♦ Maria Medina and Red Cloud; Strong Finish; Eyes front; Maria Medina; Yvette Patterson: Courtesy of Texas Tech University Sports Communications
♦ Ready to Race: Courtesy of the Estate of Jarvis Scott

Chapter 4

♦ Coach Fred T. Jones: Courtesy of the Estate of Fred T. Jones??
♦ Reynaldo Brown and Martha Watson: Courtesy of U.S. Olympic & Paralympic Committee Archives
♦ Jarvis and Barb; Friendship beyond borders; Madeline at Aztec; Bonding to enhance: Courtesy of the Estate of Jarvis Scott

Chapter 6

♦ Doris Brown, 1968 and Pan Am Games, 1967: Courtesy of U.S. Olympic & Paralympic Committee Archives
♦ Pan Am Games: Courtesy of U.S. Olympic & Paralympic Committee

- ✦ Write the vision: Courtesy of the Estate of Jarvis Scott
- ✦ Georgianna Jones at practice: Courtesy of Texas Tech University Sports Communications
- ✦ Determined to reach goals and Excited about the journey: Courtesy of the Estate of Jarvis Scott

Chapter 7

- ✦ Jarvis Scott 1968 team headshot: Courtesy of U.S. Olympic & Paralympic Committee Archives
- ✦ Ready to represent: Courtesy of the Estate of Jarvis Scott

Chapter 8

- ✦ Plan the work: Courtesy of the Estate of Jarvis Scott
- ✦ 1968 Olympic photos: Courtesy of Clarkson Creative Photography

Chapter 9

- ✦ New city: Courtesy of Texas Tech University Sports Communications
- ✦ Ready for take-off and Styling: Courtesy of the Estate of Jarvis Scott
- ✦ Jennifer Perdue Courtesy of Texas Tech University Sports Communications

Chapter 10

- ✦ Trusted delegate Jan Chesbro: Courtesy of Texas Tech University Sports Communications
- ✦ Reunited: Courtesy of Amanda Banks; Motivated to move: Courtesy of Texas Tech University Sports Communications

Chapter 11

- ✦ Kelly Malacara; Texas Tech University Head Coach, Corky Oglesby; Texas Tech Assistant Men's Coach, Abe Brown; Attention to detail: Courtesy of Texas Tech University Sports Communications; Pushing through: Courtesy of the Estate of Jarvis Scott

Chapter 12

- ✦ Audrey "Mickey" Patterson: Courtesy of the Estate of Audrey "Mickey" Patterson; Mentoring matters; Wilma Rudolph and Maria Medina: Courtesy of the Estate of Jarvis Scott ; Headshots of Audrey "Mickey" Patterson and Wilma Rudolph: Courtesy of U.S. Olympic & Paralympic Committee Archives

Chapter 13

- ✦ Proof that women coach's matter; Ronnie Green headshot, Leonard Harrison headshot: Courtesy of Texas Tech University Sports Communications; Leonard Harrison Premier: Courtesy of the Estate of Jarvis Scott

Chapter 14

* Building confidence: Courtesy of Texas Tech University Sports Communications
* Sister friend: Courtesy of Gladys Williams
* Sister friends: Courtesy of Cathy Pope
* Celebrating award: Courtesy of Amanda Banks
* Wedding pic: Courtesy of Lacey Greene
* All that I am: Courtesy of the Estate of Jarvis Scott

Chapter 16

* Jarvis and Beale at Mae Simmons Park: Courtesy of Texas Tech University Sports Communications
* Rosalyn Bryant Cal State: Courtesy of Cal State LA Athletics
* Rosalyn Bryant beads and Mae Simmons Park: Courtesy of the Estate of Jarvis Scott

Chapter 17

* Thank you for being a friend and coach: Courtesy of the Estate of Jarvis Scott; Jarvis and Michele jogging: Courtesy of Cal State LA Athletics; Martha Watson: Courtesy of U.S. Olympic & Paralympic Committee Archives; Michele Hopper, Sharon Moultrie and Motivated to Mentor: Courtesy of the Estate of Jarvis Scott; Jeannine McHaney, Sheryl Estes and Nancy King: Courtesy of Texas Tech University Sports Communications

Chapter 18

* Jarvis Scott: Courtesy of Amanda Banks

Miscellaneous Photos

* Amanda Banks: Ode to Jarvis Scott photo Courtesy of Pamela Tuckey Photography
* Author photo: Courtesy of Pamela Tuckey Photograpy

Made in the USA
Coppell, TX
03 September 2022

82501386R00144